TS

WARNING: Contains graphic depictions of trauma, terrorism, violence, injury, death and suicide.

AUTHOR'S NOTE: Some spellings of names and organisations throughout the book are different due to discrepancies in some reports.

BACK FROM THE DEAD

To Gem

BACK FROM THE DEAD

DAN BIDDLE
with Douglas Thompson

MIRROR BOOKS

m
B

MIRROR BOOKS

1

Published in Great Britain and Ireland in 2025 by
Mirror Books, a Reach PLC business.

www.mirrorbooks.co.uk
@TheMirrorBooks

Print ISBN 9781915306968
eBook ISBN 9781917439558

Cover Design: James Macey
Editing and Production: Christine Costello

Photographic acknowledgements: Alamy Dan Biddle Personal
Collection

Every effort has been made to trace copyright, Any oversights
will be rectified in future editions.

Printed and bound in Great Britain by
CPI Group (UK) Ltd, Croydon, CR0 4YY

MIX
Paper | Supporting
responsible forestry
FSC
www.fsc.org
FSC® C013604

'Io non mori', e non rimasi vivo.'
['I did not die, yet nothing of life remained.']
– **DANTE, INFERNO XXXIV**

"You can map out a fight plan or a life plan, but when the action starts, it may not go the way you planned, and you're down to your reflexes – that means your preparation. That's where your roadwork shows. If you cheated on that in the dark of the morning, well, you're going to get found out now, under the bright lights."

– JOE FRAZIER, 1970

UNDER THE BRIGHT LIGHTS

TONY ADAMS MBE

DAN'S STORY OF SUPERHUMAN fortitude in the face of unimaginable horror is both gripping and terrifying. Yet every page glows with his warmth, humour and positivity as he discovers a life of love and understanding with an unquenchable faith in humanity. Inspirational doesn't do him justice.

It is with great honour that I write this foreword to Dan's book. A man who has lived through the incomprehensible physical, mental and emotional trauma of the 7/7 bombings and has now come out the other side and managed to turn the unimaginable into the redemptive. It is a story of courage, fear, despair, love, joy and surrender. He shows us all how, after years of mental and physical therapy, and with the fearless support of his partner by his side, he has turned the near life-ending injuries into the positives of work, life and relationships.

I first met Dan through listening to him – his powerful message is articulated brilliantly in his talks. And in this written account, Dan explores further the physical and philosophical pitfalls as well as mental and moral opportunities as he faces them. He now works tirelessly for disability access and processes and with me in the mental health arena. This lust for life – and to help others – is paramount to who he is. You will read here the story of one man's battle against the odds, but you will also read of a man of integrity, determination, gentleness, humility, pride, warmth and unimpeachable good nature. I defy you not to cry – but tears of joy, not sadness. It is a tale that must be told. And it is a tale that must be read to be believed.

Introduction

TO HELL AND BACK

'It is love, not reason, that is stronger than death.'
– THOMAS MANN, THE MAGIC MOUNTAIN, 1924

FOR SUCH A LONG time living was a fate worse than death for Dan Biddle.

In a moment of someone else's madness, he lost all meaning to his existence, along with both his legs, his left eye, his spleen and all hearing in his left ear.

His body and mind were devastated on 7 July 2005, during the worst single terrorist atrocity on British soil. It took ten seconds to disassemble him. It took much longer, nearly 90 pints of blood – that's more than ten body refills – and exceptional medical expertise to put some of him back together again.

Dan was the most injured person in the explosions which murdered 52 people and left 748 other victims wounded on 7/7/2005, the first suicide bomber attacks in the UK.

Today a 20 pence piece, which punctured his leg like a

bullet, remains lodged in his thigh bone and the face and actions of suicide bomber Mohammad Sidique Khan are as permanently wedged inside his mind. His image often arrives at his home at bedtime and stays until breakfast. On cruel days, he's there just in time for tea.

Khan's body was ripped apart and scattered all about London's Edgware Road Tube station by the home-made bomb he set off inside his rucksack. Yet, with haphazard happenstance, a sudden noise, the slam of a car door, the smell of burned toast, the hiss of steam in a coffee shop, Khan is back beside Dan.

Dan can't escape Khan. He appears at the best and worst times. Exclusive to him. There's no editing him out of his life for he's there, inside his head. Awake or asleep, the pernicious Khan will sneak into the moment and Dan is back on that morning Tube, at 8.52 am, in the tunnel, the noise, the bedlam and the burning and the death, all noxious and overwhelming, and smothering the will to live on.

Khan, like the pain Dan suffers from his lost legs, is phantom but, again like the pain, so real to Dan that the agony and terror are equally so.

This is Dan Biddle's story of his survival but, like no other, it is the testimony of his fight with Complex Post Traumatic Stress Disorder (CPTSD), something much mis-understood and rarely discussed. The mundane acronym disguises the anguish of this most extreme form of PTSD which hurtles Dan into constant recreations of the day the man he used to be died. It is not a flashback to Dan. His mind insists he is there.

It's *Groundhog Day* as a horror movie.

A harrowing account of physical and emotional survival against a diverse and exhausting catalogue of anguish at official blunders, of suicide attempts, frustration and anger, lost and found love, a remarkable capacity for innovation, and, he says, the bloody-mindedness of a good Essex boy which helps contain the demons which haunt him from moment to moment.

It is also the disquieting disclosure of what happens to the victims in the aftermath of natural and man-made disasters, after the fanfare of fascination and concern around our shock dissipates and, shamefully, interest and information disappears. There are always warm words for the survivors of such horrors, inspirational reports and comfort headlines, but little focus on the day-to-day of being damaged but alive, going to the bathroom, making a cup of tea. The despair may become less intense, the sense of shock might diminish, but neither vanishes, although life prevails.

Dan's testimony is the reality after you and your life are blown to bits.

Douglas Thompson, Suffolk, England,
February 2025

Prologue

UNCIVIL SERVICE

'Truth is the daughter of Time.'
– ANCIENT PROVERB

1 NOVEMBER 2005

THE GREAT AND GOOD gathered at St Paul's Cathedral. The Queen, the Duke of Edinburgh, Prime Minister Tony Blair, the Deputy Prime Minister, the Chancellor of the Exchequer, the Leader of the Opposition, and the Archbishop of Canterbury, who told the congregation:

'Time gives perspective and may bring healing, but the trauma of violence, makes a difference that nothing will ever completely unmake.'

Which is a long way of saying when you're blown to bits you get fucked up. A lack of brevity from the Archbishop, but spot on, nevertheless.

Full on agree with that, yet the words fell downwards like

the gaze of most of the congregation that day. It was like they'd gone to a freak show, and they didn't want to look at the exhibits. I was sitting uncomfortably in my wheel-chair, my brother Tony next to me, in an alcove of Wren's cathedral. With us were other survivors who had lost limbs and bits of sanity and around them the friends and relatives of those who lost their lives in the criminally misguided name of somebody else's God.

As I sat and watched I was angry. Not at that moment at the bombers, although that fury will never go away, but at the politicians. They'd put us in the corner of the cathedral, like naughty boys, as far away from the Queen and the others as possible; they shuffled us out of sight, tucked up so that when the politicians left, they wouldn't see us. The Queen and Prince Philip went out a side entrance and when Blair was about to walk out my brother said: 'This is disgusting, he should see the catastrophe he caused.'

The horror stories flashed through my mind. Not just my pain and agonies. There was a lot of hell that day. One victim had somebody's hand surgically removed from their leg. They had been sitting next to each other and the blast had blown the hand off and through the guy's leg.

Another man was blown in half and that inferno heat welded his top half to the floor of the carriage; his body had been cauterised. I watched as rescuers lifted him and dislodged the seal and his intestines fell out. Behind him another man was waving his arms and screaming his wife's name and burning to death.

10

A girl who got out of her bombed carriage, climbed up onto the platform and started walking to work. A fireman grabbed her and said she had to sit down but she kept saying she was fine. She was in complete shock. She didn't realise she had the Tube seat hanging out of her. It had been blasted right into her, cut through her and here she was bleeding and bleeding, almost dead and climbing up the steps and trying to go to work. How could that be?

I understand that now. I never would have before 7/7.

The things your brain does to you when you think you're going to die. It is unbelievable, unless you've gone through it. Which is why, at times, it might be difficult for me to explain, so you can fully comprehend, the trauma. I'll try my best. Beware, it's not popcorn and special effects. It's real.

At St Paul's, as flashbacks swelled in my head, I told my brother to get out of the effin' way and I wheeled right to the end of the area where Blair couldn't miss me. I stared at him, but he walked on, looking at the ground. He wouldn't look at me. It was just inhumane the way he acted. He wasn't going to speak to us, look at us, we were these people who weren't worthy of his time. I looked at him and thought: 'This is partly on you, you bastard, and you can't even look at what your errors have caused.' He didn't have the decency to look at me.

It may sound cynical but I can't help feeling that if everyone had been killed on 7/7 it might have been dismissed as three electrical faults on the Tube and an engine explosion on the bus.

11

It wouldn't have been put across as a terrorist attack if there had been no survivors or witnesses. They would have covered up the first suicide attack on Britain.

The powers that be have certainly let it fade into history.

About a month before I got the hump with Tony Blair and his lot at St Paul's, a nice fella from the police came to see me in hospital. He was a little tongue-tied. He was nervous and I felt sorry for him, and I asked him: 'You all right, mate?'

He'd asked me a few questions and now he said to me: 'I've got to ask you a question and, to be honest with you, I don't know how to do it so you'll have to forgive me as the only way is to ask you straight out.'

'Crack on,' I told him.

'Outside, guarded by two other officers, I've got your legs. What do you want me to do with them?'

'You've got my what?'

'We have your legs. We've finished with them evidentially. Do you want 'em?'

I said: 'What do you mean, do I want them? You fucking kidding me?

'I want them attached. I don't want them as an ornament.'

He looked crestfallen so I laughed and that helped him. He said they had to ask as some victims wanted to see them and say goodbye to their bits and pieces. He said they had my legs in the mortuary, and he could take me down there to see them if that's what I wanted. Or I had to fill out some forms and they'd forensically dispose of them.

It was my right leg, right foot and then the bit just below my knee above where they'd amputated, so there was a chunk of it and then it was my left leg and left foot which had been separated in the blast and I had to sign for each bit to be destroyed.

I also had to sign for my eye to be destroyed, well, what was left of my eye. They had it all for evidence. I had to give them permission to destroy it and that was some eerie and recurring nightmare scenario.

By then they'd got all the evidence they needed, bits of the train, bits of the bomb, bits of Christ knows what and clearly bits of me. They'd done all they could with it, they'd forensically swiped it for the chemical makeup of the bomb as well. They'd done what they needed to do. They just didn't need these bits of me anymore. I did. But there was 'eff all I could do with them. Superglue only goes so far.

Along with some puzzled doctors uncomprehending at my win against all odds, and medical science, I remain amazed that I survived. I often feel guilt for that, another ongoing 7/7 curse I can do nothing about. Yet, I pledged to myself that day in St Paul's that when I felt physically and, most importantly, completely mentally stable, I would tell my story which, well, is the story of me and Khan. And the bomb.

Don't expect frills, tales of some jolly disabled survivor who learned to skydive or conquer Everest. The tourist traps of tragedy were and are beyond me.

This is not a miracle story. There were, and still are,

crucial and daily challenges. It's taken me many years to get it together and be able to carry on living. That's what it's all about for all of us.

I'll crack on with it.

PART ONE
THE BOMBS

'Mr Biddle, the words "if only" must resound… you have suffered so much, and your survival is inspirational.'
– LADY JUSTICE HALLET, CORONER'S INQUESTS

Prelude

PREMEDITATED

*'How well I have learned that there is no fence to sit on
between Heaven and Hell... that chasm is no place
for any man.'*
– JOHNNY CASH, 1981.

SYLVIA WAUGH WAKES UP at 3.46am – she looks at
her bedside clock – on 7 July 2005, disturbed by three men
noisily talking outside her bedroom window in Alexandra
Grove, Leeds. She parts her net curtains and sees the men
load black rucksacks into the boot of a blue Nissan Micra,
assuming they're drug dealing in the public car park.

Suddenly, a man turns and looks straight at her. She
jumps back from the window in fright. Her sleepy husband
mumbles: 'That's what you get for being nosy.'

Mrs Waugh sees the beginning of a five-hour journey
which ends in Britain's first suicide bomb attack murdering
52 people and ruining the lives of so many more.

The men that she witnesses set off down the M1 toward

Luton to join up with the fourth bomber, 19-year-old Germaine Lindsay, are Mohammad Sidique Khan, 30, Shehzad Tanweer, 22, and Hasib Hussain, 18.

Stopping at Woodhall Spa services for petrol, the three bombers buy a breakfast of Ginsters cheese and onion slices, Walkers crisps and Volvic mineral water.

Germaine Lindsay waits for them in his Fiat Brava at Luton station. He's calm, he falls asleep and gets a parking ticket at 5.53am. Together they board the Thameslink 7.25am train to London King's Cross; other passengers notice they're wearing overcoats, strangely overdressed for summer. Barrister Ben Leech assumes they're off on holiday as two of them are 'sharing a joke, laughing, smiling and generally relaxing'.

When they arrive at King's Cross at 8.23am and separate, ready to explode evil across the city's public transport system, most of their victims are going to work on the London Tube and buses.

Chapter One

SLIDING DOORS

'You often meet your fate on the road you take to avoid it.'
— *FRENCH PROVERB*

WHAT IF? A QUESTION for the rest of my life.

I nearly didn't go to work that Thursday morning. I had a splitting headache, not one self-inflicted in the pub, but a howling migraine.

It had been a long Wednesday, a real fanfare of a day. London was announced as host city for the Olympic Games, a hat trick following 1908 and 1948, to be in held in 2012. I was construction manager on a building job at a mental health centre in Wembley, north London, a fair trek for me living out east in Upminster. I was also mentoring a new lad, a trainee named Ollie. When the Olympic news came in, the nurses and patients cheered. It was a smiling, happy day.

I love my sport, and it was one of those proud didn't-we-do-well moments when you feel clever for simply being alive. And the prospect of that Olympic-sized building work. Bonanza. That evening, I was in goal, at 19-stone, 6ft 4in tall, nifty at keeping the ball out of the net, for my semi-pro team Interlink FC. I can still *see* myself that evening: big, strong, enjoying life. I still inhabit the vital moments of Thursday 7/7 in the present tense.

****

I sleep like a log but wake up with my 5am alarm and a pneumatic drill digging a road from my forehead through the back of my head. My vision is dodgy and I feel groggy. Maybe I'll take the day off. I stay in bed and close my eyes and sleep on fitfully for half an hour.

Feeling a little better, the pain in my head easing, and not wanting to leave Ollie stranded on the big job on his own, I decide to go in. I'm running about an hour late, but I get my arse in gear, speed shower, dress in the usual clobber, jeans, T-shirt, Caterpillar boots, thinking: *Better late than never.* Sod's Law, when you're up against the clock, time conspires against you. A burst water main on Clockhouse Lane slows up my 248 bus to Romford mainline station. I think about running up the road to the house to get my car and driving in. I don't.

At Romford the automated ticket machine in the foyer of the station isn't working; I queue at the ticket office, lose more time as it's now rush hour, and the station is jam-packed. But time to moan to myself about the 12 quid for a Travelcard to take me roundtrip to Wembley Central. And the all stops train – somewhere is warning me and I'm not receiving – is delayed, a signal failure at Stratford. Typical London Transport.

Finally, we stop-go rattle into Liverpool Street station and I constantly check the time. There's more rush hour delay. I race through the station to the Circle line but the first westbound Tube I need for Baker Street, to change to the Bakerloo line for Wembley is rammed, every carriage like a giant sardine tin. With my dodgy head I can't face it.

The next one takes an age, loads of District Line trains, but not my boy. Finally, finally, one shows up. I usually park myself at the back of the Tube because you never hear of a train reversing into something. I'm rushing, I get on the second carriage at the front, and stand right by the doors. I lean against the Perspex at the entrance. The carriage isn't overly busy. I'm anxious about being late, especially as I'm training Ollie up as a site manager with me.

My idea is to put a text message into my phone, get off the train at Baker Street, dash outside the station for a signal and send the text message and let Ollie know I'm running late. But I'm all thumbs on this Nokia 33 and with the bumping Tube, I make a meal of getting the message done. I'm so busy typing the text I miss my stop.

We come into Edgware Road, and I look up at the Tube map and it's okay as I can pick up the Bakerloo at the next station, Paddington.

At Edgware Road, passengers get off, others come on, the usual impatient crush. It's busy but not jammed. I check my watch, it's a bit slow, and see it's 8.50am. We move into the tunnel, head into Paddington and, as the train turns on the bend in the tunnel, I look at the fella sitting next to me. He leans forward, glances along the carriage, sits back a little bit and stares at me.

There's a girl near him and her MP3 is playing 'Professional Widow' by Tori Amos loudly and it's hurting my sore head. It irritates me.

The beginning of the end of my life as I know it starts here.

I don't know if it's subliminal, maybe call it past life memory, but I see Mohammad Sidique Khan, sitting calmly in his green jacket, faded not bright, and his watch, expensive and below the cuff on his left hand, and his off-white baseball cap and, of course, the rucksack-type backpack in his lap on the end of the bank of seats just behind the Perspex. I don't think anything of him.

I watched Khan get on the train, he boarded at King's Cross and once on the train he walked the length of the carriage, spent 30-40 seconds at the far end of the train, then proceeded to come back to where I was stood and occupied the seat next to me. He is no more than six inches away from me, his rucksack on his lap in line with my knees as I am stood next to him.

He looks up at me but quickly lowers his eyes and puts his right hand through the zip in the top of his bag and explodes himself in a white light all across, right and left, up and down and below the carriage in a kaleidoscopic fury. Bits of me follow as the explosion violently opens the carriage doors and, just as violently and God Almightily, maliciously rockets me up to the roof of the carriage. The carriage's hand pole spears me and – I now know – punctures my colon, rupturing my spleen and bowel. I bounce down and out through the gap where the Tube doors were and, headfirst, ricochet off the Tube tunnel wall. I skid along and land on my back next to the tracks and the gravel cuts into me, sharp little knives, little buggers, stabbing me and something that feels like a brick is prodding into me. I'm fully conscious. It's hot. The Tube train gives an eerie wheeze and halts, abruptly as if hitting the proverbial brick wall. There's a terrific groan. And a chilling scream, a subterranean echo: I'm the one screaming.

I'm dying a thousand deaths a second. The pain, the pain, and then whatever feeling there is vanishes as if with the click of a switch. And the awful mind-warping claustrophobia. Even in this darkness I make things out; it's not pitch black. There's so much smoke and dust and the first 30 or 40 seconds is an eternity after the blast, for there's silence. Limbo, like the end of the world. A trance. It's as if all life is dumbstruck, thinking: *What the fuck happened here?*

That silence, and then someone makes a noise, a squeal, and the gates of Hell open up. The sound is phenomenal, and horror comes from every angle. It's spooky. The sounds, the smells, the heat, burning heat, and the filth of it with the rats and spiders disturbed by the destruction and crawling all over me. It's as if Dracula is conjuring.

My body, what's left of it, points toward Edgware Road,

and my arms are in the surrender position. As I lay there the very train I have just been so violently ejected from, continues moving and I see the huge wheel on the track approaching me, I shut my eyes thinking it was going to cut me in half, but nothing, I open my eyes and the wheel is coming to a stop just up from where my head lay.

It's dark but there's some light. It's from me. I'm on fire. Around my stomach there's flames. I move my neck enough to see my arms are being barbecued. My arms swell and my watch is red hot, and the steel strap cuts into my ballooning arm and sizzles my skin. I tear it off and drop it on the tracks and flap my arms to put out the flames. I try and move and realise I'm pinned down by heaps of mangled metal, the Tube carriage door. I can't move it with my arms. And I can't feel my legs. I can't lever with them. The left leg is gone above the knee, the right leg is shredded and faces down instead of up, blown round 180 degrees. Lying on your back, your toes should be in the air – I'm on my back and my toes dig into the ground.

As the dust and smoke clears, I see bodies and body parts all around me. I put my hand on my forehead, and it goes inside my head and runs up and down, zigzagging like Harry Potter's scar, and touches the bone of my skull. My eardrums are burst, but I hear muffled shouting and screaming. The screaming is incessant, it's like people gargling with death.

There's a girl lying behind me, we are head to head and I can see the catastrophic injuries which have left her dead –

since that moment my recurring nightmare is her crawling up my bed screaming at me to help her, shouting: 'It's your fault, why didn't you help me?'

When screams suddenly stop I know someone has died. Like the cauterised man blown in half. I try again to move the train doors off my legs, but putting my hands underneath is like sticking them into a bucket of papier-mâché. Something digs in my back. I pull it out and it's a foot, in a black brogue shoe with a purple, red and gold Pringle sock on it.

I'm sure I'm dying down there in that hellhole, no lingering illusions. Yet, I shout for help. I'm fearful, not of dying but dying on my own, and being an anonymous body in a bag, like someone's used laundry. In death I don't want to be alone. I'm losing a lot of blood. I'm 26 years old and I'm thinking: *I'm going to die down here and there's nothing I can do about it. There's nothing that is going to change the fact that I'm going to die in this dirty, shitty Underground tunnel.*

I accept it and it calms me down. But my brain does the evil trick and makes me think about the things I'm going to miss; my life flashes before my eyes, fast, like a Formula One car, punishing me with all the things I'm not going to ever do, the life I've never had, the life I'm losing.

But. But. I'm clinging on because I need somebody to know who I am, how old I am, I need somebody to tell my parents and everyone else I love that I'm thinking of them. I can't see my injuries with the train doors on top of me but I know it's really bad and I think to myself: I don't want my dad to see this. My dad doesn't need to walk into a room and see his son dead looking like this and that to be his last memory of me.

I'm in terror of dying alone. I scream for help: 'Please help me, for God's sake somebody help me, somebody get me out of here.' I'm in the throes of dying, I scream my head off in a panic that I'm going to die alone, thinking I'm within 20 seconds of death. People scream in horror films and actors give it a real go but hearing it for real, there's nothing that compares to absolute abject terror. Which is what those moments are for me.

I'd last seen my dad in April at a posh golf club in Spain and I want that, us in the sun with a beer in our hands and laughing, for if there is such a place as hell on earth that's where I am. I'm screaming and I'm tiring when I hear a deep South African voice say: 'My name's Adrian… don't worry, I've been in this situation before. I'll get you out.'

He's with another fella, Lee Hunt, and Adrian tells me: 'Hold Lee's hand.'

'Why's that?' I ask.

'Because this is going to fucking hurt. Brace yourself, mate.'

Shit, it can get worse?

I grip Lee's hand but feel nothing. Adrian is a giant of a guy and is risking electrocution getting onto the track and crawling under the train. Lee Hunt, an Underground driver on a tea break at Edgware Road depot, risks his life too. Adrian tells me he is a security specialist and works as a bodyguard and talks, talks, to distract me. He pushes his hand into what's left of my leg and roots around to find the femoral artery with his fingers and pinches it shut, my life truly in his hand. He holds the life into me. Lee shines a torch in my eyes to make me blink and stay awake and they talk to me about football, about Arsenal being my favourite team, about me being a sportsman and a goalkeeper, about my family, about anything so I will stay awake. So I will stay alive.

Help arrives after 40 minutes, the rescuers went to the wrong entrance due to a miscommunication and I'm conscious, looking at the Tube tunnel wall with a big white painted 4 on it. I'm not feeling it, but blood is pumping into me and I'm moving on a stretcher. Adrian and Lee are with me, talking to me.

The Tube driver meets us. He won't leave until the last surviving passenger is out – 'They're my responsibility'– and I'm lifted over the ticket barrier and up the stairs and out to the ambulance… it's all lights and sirens and pandemonium. And the smell of smoke, of burning, of disaster, a symphony of confusion and hysteria. My memory banks it all. The injured pull bits of metal from themselves and people climb out of the carriage, being sick, crying and all sorts and it's a cacophony of sound that's never left me. People tussle to get around us, get safe.

One thing I'm holding onto is that in the space of minutes I'm facing the worst of humanity – and the best. Adrian is my first miracle.

In the ambulance I can't get my breath, my asthma adds torment, it's as though a weight holds it inside me, and a paramedic tries to put an oxygen mask on me. Jesus, the pain on my burned face. I scream at him; I can't take any more pain. I get them to move the stretcher to breathe better. The ambulance pulls into the emergency bay and the driver clips the kerb and the paramedic with me shouts: 'This guy's got enough to contend with, you dickhead, do you have to hit the kerb?'

I'm the first survivor into St Mary's Hospital, Paddington. The doctor looks at me with utter panic, no idea where to start with this horror show. My barbecued arms are five times their normal size, like the Michelin Balloon man. My legs, what is left of them, are mangled and cut and I'm bleeding all over. My left eye isn't there and my house keys and money, £7.40 in loose change, are embedded in my body along with bits of flying glass and metal from the tunnel. Of course, with all that and my skull half open, I'm in a state. In front of me is a chorus line of doctors and consultants. What is my name? I know that and say it.

Yet, the look of 'em, they don't think I'll last the night, but at the same time I know they'll do their best. I don't really know why but I think, like me, they're sticking two fingers up at the bombers.

That said, it doesn't start well. The surgeon is telling me he's going to take great care of me, and, in a flick of time, it's lights out, it's goodbye. I die on them.

Chapter Two

STAYIN' ALIVE

'I'll be back.'
– Arnold Schwarzenegger, The Terminator, 1984

AT ACCIDENT AND EMERGENCY, the medics immediately gave me a sedative. It, in turn, gave me a heart attack. I'd lost so much blood there was more sedation fluid
than blood in me. When this dose hit my heart, I had a
cardiac arrest and effectively died. They resuscitated me.
My heart stopped again on the scanning machine. I died
again. They brought me back one more time.

It was like a run on a brewery the way they were pouring
pints of blood into me. About an hour or so into the
operation my heart stopped once more, and it wasn't so
easy to revive me; they couldn't restart my heart with a
defibrillator or adrenaline shot. They'd had their chance at
that. It wasn't feasible.

I've a scar on my chest where they opened me up, broke
some ribs and a surgeon put her hands, magic fingers, into

my chest and manually pumped my heart. She kept the blood flowing oxygen to it. But I'm dead, well dead. All the machines say I'm dead and the medics are going with that. No need for VAR.

The surgeon, a real heroine, never stopped working, massaging my heart. The doctors are looking at their watches. At 15 minutes they're obliged to make it official that I'm a goner. But my heart came back to me. The hands-on doctor had nine seconds left when my heart began beating on its own. Not a thump. A flutter. That was good enough for them – and for me.

I woke up eight weeks later. And started putting together the story of what happened to me and others on that day, on that 7/7, and being astonished at being alive. I still am.

Cats have nine lives. I'm giving them a bit of a run. I've died three times on an operating table – tops they gave me a two percent chance of living – and had the same number of goes at killing myself. The doctors were brilliant at saving my life and I was crap at ending it. Some skill sets you don't want.

Today I'm alive and accept who I have become. I live in parallel worlds. I'm married and madly in love with my wife. But there will always be a third person in our marriage. Khan is always sneaking around threatening to destroy what we have. I needed to study and know him. He's my shadow, something I can't escape but I defy every day. He stole from me and all my anger is devoted to getting what I can back.

Today my brain processes normal as dangerous because getting on a train and going to work is normal, getting on the train and standing next to a guy with a bomb who tries to kill you is not; my brain now dictates normal activities as being dangerous. It's one of the many things that I strive to control, but every time I go out of the house, there's an intake of breath, the abject terror of going outside.

I left my house on 7 July 2005 at half past six in the morning a fit, able, strong man, but I didn't come home that way. It wasn't like I went to war or anything like that. I was going to a building site and somebody tried to kill me. So nothing I ever do now feels safe.

They're matter of fact, the details, when turned into statistics, but what Khan and his cohorts did that day continues to plague me.

When I was rescued, six other victims* lay dead near me. Another passenger, Catherine Al-Wafai, said our carriage went completely dark. She has memories like mine: 'I will recall the smell of smoke forever. I could hear people screaming. I remember a strong smell of burning and having difficulty breathing. It was chaos inside the carriage. The lady to my left was not moving. She had blood spouting from her. The blood saturated my clothing.'

In East London, a Circle line train driven by Timothy Batkin was crammed with people who had switched from delayed trains on the Bakerloo line.

About 100 yards into the tunnel toward Aldgate station, he felt 'a powerful thud'. Shehzad Tanweer had detonated the first bomb, killing seven people. The driver heard people crying for help: 'It was a chilling, haunting cry that still makes my blood run cold.'

Mr Batkin used his mobile phone, which worked because the line was close to the surface, to tell the line manager there had been an explosion. Dazed passengers began stumbling onto the track, bloodied and with their clothes shredded.

Within three minutes of the Aldgate and Edgware Road explosions, teenager Germaine Lindsay detonated his bomb on a Piccadilly line train between King's Cross and Russell Square, killing 26 people.

The emergency services were alerted after Mr Batkin's call to London Underground staff at Aldgate. The first reports of incidents at Aldgate and Edgware Road were received at the Network Control Centre of London Underground at 8.52am. By 9.03am a station manager at Edgware Road was saying 'something has gone badly wrong…'

The Aldgate station manager, Celia Harrison, did not tell the control room there might have been an explosion because she did not want to cause panic. Convinced they were dealing with an electrical surge, the control room sent technical experts to Aldgate to deal with the problem.

It was the first of countless delays that left hundreds of people in spiralling pain and bewilderment. At Liverpool Street, where staff heard the Aldgate explosion, managers became tangled up in procedure. Because of fears of more bombs, they were stopped by British Transport Police from going into the tunnel. It was nearly half an hour after the blast when they officially went in. Some exceptionally brave guys had ignored the dangers and gone in to help. The managers set up a whiteboard to list their team's names and equipment before sending them into the tunnel.

As dozens of 999 calls came into the London Ambulance Service control room, chaos took hold. Only one person was logging all the emergency calls. Vital information was written on scraps of paper.

The worker updating information on the whiteboard was only tall enough to reach halfway up it.

It all led to delays in getting ambulances to assist. At King's Cross, paramedics arrived about 9.14am, nearly half an hour after the explosion. There was another half-hour delay before they went underground as they treated the walking wounded.

At Aldgate, firemen cursed at the first ambulance staff to arrive because they refused to take survivors to hospital, saying they had to assess all victims.

One lost his temper telling a paramedic: 'Give me the fucking keys and I will drive the fucking ambulance.'

Paramedics were not the only emergency workers hampered by official procedures. Some firemen refused to enter the Tube tunnels until they were assured the electricity was switched off. At Aldgate, Inspector Robert Munn stood on the power rail to prove it was switched off. But fire crew said they needed confirmation from Underground staff. The delays left scores of survivors having to do whatever they could to help the injured and dying.

Elizabeth Kenworthy, an off-duty police officer, was in the fourth carriage of the Aldgate train. She ran towards the bomb carriage, where she saved the life of the now renowned Paralympian Martine Wright MBE (who was a member of the sitting volleyball team in 2012) by using her jacket as a tourniquet on the stumps of her legs.

'I wouldn't even describe it as a tourniquet. It was more of a dressing to stop her from bleeding to death,' she recalled.

Constable Kenworthy assumed help would soon be at hand, but like countless other survivors, she became increasingly alarmed by the inexplicable delays. 'I looked at my watch after I had done the initial first aid. I looked at 9.05, then I looked at 9.10. By 9.20 I was starting to think: "Where are they?"'

Paul Glennerster, whose leg was blown off, was convinced nobody would come to rescue him. 'I decided to get out. I picked my leg up and hopped.'

At Edgware Road, Jason Rennie ignored his own injuries and tried to help Stan Brewster, who was lodged in the hole in the floor left by the bomb: 'He had his hand out and was asking to be assisted to get out of the hole. I walked slowly forward and grabbed his hand. I had difficulty keeping my footing because there was so much blood. Moments later, Mr Brewster died.'

Emergency workers finally began to arrive in the carriages about half an hour after the bombs went off, but nobody was prepared for the scenes that confronted them deep underground.

At King's Cross, Peter Taylor, the first paramedic in the tunnel, faced 'mounds of bodies and dismembered limbs' as he entered the bomb carriage. Some victims were still moving. One man was crying out 'help me' but by the time he reached him he was dead. Emergency crews were overwhelmed by the carnage. Neil Walker, a fireman, said the bandages in his small first aid kit ran out quickly. He 'watched a young man die' while he was waiting for paramedics to arrive at Aldgate.

With no radio or mobile phone coverage underground, emergency workers sent runners to and from the surface with updates and requests for equipment.

Yet amid the horror, there were tales of extraordinary good fortune. Philip Duckworth was standing so close to Tanweer that he was blinded in one eye by a splinter from the bomber's shin bone. But he lived. After being thrown on to the tracks, he heard a rescuer say: 'This one's gone'.

He said: 'At that point I was like, "No I'm not, hang on a second, I'm not gone" and I forced myself on to my knees.'

Suicide bomber Hasib Hussain failed to detonate his device and left the Tube at King's Cross after his bomb failed. He bought a new battery at a WHSmith store and boarded a No 91 bus. It's so mundane, terrifying. Anita Dybek-Echtermeyer was on that bus and said Hussain's bag looked heavy: 'He had sweat going onto his chin, dry, white lips, he looked nervous and exhausted.'

The bus stopped at Euston as the authorities began to close off London, which by now was on terror alert; mobile phone service was down, the Internet was being monitored, the skies patrolled by fighter planes and electronically. Downing Street was on high alert.

Hussain switched to a Number 30 bus [from Marble Arch to Hackney Wick] that headed south into Tavistock Square. He set off his bomb toward the rear of the top deck, killing 13 people. By sheer chance the bus had blown up outside the headquarters of the British Medical Association [BMA]. Doctors rushed out and used tablecloths, jackets and ties as bandages.

Dr Anthony Everington, a GP and former BMA deputy chairman, said he was met by 'a funny mix of quietness, stillness, a few sirens in the background, pigeons cooing' while all around him people lay injured or dead.

The first ambulance to arrive at Tavistock Square did so only by chance. Ambulance drivers Jessica Ashford and Nadene Conway had been sent to King's Cross but came across the bus at 9.57am, about ten minutes after the blast. They asked for backup, but the first ambulances were only dispatched at 10.42am and did not arrive for another ten minutes – an hour after the explosion. By now the other injured were arriving at London hospitals, while other survivors stumbled their way home in a daze. Catherine Al-Wafai, who was on my train, walked home without realising she was missing a shoe.

I was missing a great deal more.

But I had a saviour, the former Army medic Adrian Heili, who later told us *his* story.

ADRIAN HEILI

'It was just going to be a normal day. I was a personal protection officer at the time and doing security chauffeuring. I was seeing friends in north London. I got off the bus at Baker Street to get on the train because I was getting off at High Street Kensington. I normally get into the second carriage but because I was running a bit late, I had to run and jump on the train so I actually got on to the third carriage. It was coming into rush hour, there must have been 60 to 70 passengers in the carriage. There weren't enough places to sit so I was standing. We went through a couple of stations and into Edgware Road. Everything seemed fine. Then about four or five seconds later, the whole train just went dark and shuddered and there was this violent shaking and flames down the side of the carriage, a lot of banging, crashing, the scraping of metal.

'I was thrown around and pieces of glass went into my head. I had two fractured ribs as well. There was this horrible smell and taste that was in the air. The whole place filled up with smoke and soot. It was hazy, really dusty and hard to see. You can smell the copper; you can smell burned electrics but then there is a sulphur smell that comes afterwards. Then I started to hear screaming from outside the carriage and that's when I heard Danny Biddle.

'I could hear people screaming and shouting but he for

me was really the loudest and I could tell he was in a lot of pain. He was shouting: "Help me, I'm bleeding."

'I went to the back of the train, and we couldn't get through the doors, eventually one of the London Underground staff came and opened them. I started walking towards the oncoming train and there were bodies. One of the images that will always stick with me is there were just bodies on the floor. There was no indication of what kind of person they were, they were just charcoal.

'When you went into the carriage there was six feet of steel missing, so there was a lot of debris. In the carriage that had been blown up, there wasn't any definition or colour. You don't have the coloured seats or anything like that, it was just charcoal all around. There was so much plastic burned and there were dead in that carriage.

'Then I made one of the hardest choices I have ever had to make. Which people was there any point in stopping and helping? You say to yourself: "Who is the worst and who can I save?" That was the hardest choice.

'As I was walking, I met a guy by the name of Lee Hunt, one of the Underground drivers, also an ex-military guy. We were making our way towards Danny Biddle because we could hear him screaming.

'I got down on my hands and knees and crawled underneath the train. When I put my hands down, I thought: "This isn't water I am putting my hands into, this is something else." When I got some light, I could see it was blood.

'When I got to Danny, a large piece of steel had landed on him – it was a Tube train door. Lee and I moved the door together. Danny was a mess.

'Danny had been blown out the door, then taken it with him and rolled along the roof.

'From where Danny's leg had been taken, there wasn't a clean cut. I put a tourniquet on one leg, which was torn at the lower part. It used my belt for that. Then I removed the remainder of the door and saw his other leg had been taken off.

'He was losing a lot of blood through his femoral artery. I grabbed the artery with my thumb and forefingers, so he didn't bleed out, tried to squeeze that as quickly and as hard as possible. I took my shirt off and built a tourniquet for his other leg. They eventually arrived with a paramedic for Danny, who did a bit more than I could. Then the fire brigade came down with a stretcher and we pulled him out...'

****

If I had any luck that day, it was Adrian Heili. He was what I needed, a guy who'd completed four tours of Kosovo with the Austrian Army, and especially his words: 'I've never lost anyone yet and I don't intend to start now.'

There have been times of great despondency when I cursed him for that but that was and is part of the devilment of PTSD.

What with his two emergency tourniquets and encouragements I truly know he saved my life that day. I was petrified beyond what I can even explain now, when Adrian found me.

I held on because I needed somebody to know me; we all want to be somebody, to be known. Being a burned bundle of flesh and blood and never identified terrorised me to my core. I needed somebody to know who *I was*.

Since that day, for 20 years, I've been trying to prove who *I am*.

Chapter Three

TO DIE ANOTHER DAY

'The suicide bomber's imagination leads him to believe in a brilliant act of heroism, when in fact he is simply blowing himself up pointlessly and taking other people's lives.'
– SALMAN RUSHDIE, 1987

I CAN REMEMBER A split second of the coma, a moment of being awake during one of the surgeries and clocking the panic on the medical team's face as my eyes opened and they knocked me out with more anaesthetic.

Comatose, I missed being a 'missing person'.

In the chaos following Khan and his lads blowing up London, I was one of so many people who couldn't be traced. I was reported to the hotline for those anxious about their relatives and loved ones. By then I was in St Mary's being kept alive by blood transfusions – the doctors couldn't stop me bleeding – and hope, and remarkable skill.

My father, John, and Pauline, my mother, were beside themselves. It was a horrific déjà vu for them. My brother

Tony was working in New York on 9/11 when Bin Laden's bunch of thugs took havoc to America with 2,996 deaths in the separate Islamist suicide terrorist attacks of September 2001. My brother was 'missing' to them for several hours before they made contact.

Now, where was I? It was all happening again. They live in Spain, so they felt more isolated from facts. The television, all the news, was flames and sirens, noise and dead and injured people. Adrian had my name and the doctors retrieved bits of a bank credit card from somewhere in my body – my London Transport Travelcard for that day remained intact in my wallet in my back pocket and I still have that morbid memento – so the emergency services contacted them.

They alerted my brother, who arrived from America before they made it from Spain. I'm big news – the most injured survivor. The newspapers were chasing my family. I'm oblivious, not even aware that I'm alive, never mind confusing all around me by surviving. If only just.

I lost three and a half pints of blood in the tunnel, and we only have eight to ten. It was gushing out from me. I was about 30 seconds away from what they call exsanguination, when you completely bleed out. Which is why when I first arrived at the hospital and the sedation drug they gave me got into my circulatory system my heart arrested and I died.

They brought me back with the paddles the first time for that. Then they sent me for a scan, and I had another massive cardiac arrest then. They brought me back from that. I was about four hours into more surgery when I had another massive cardiac arrest. That was because they were trying to stop the bleeding from my legs and the cardiothoracic surgeon who was in the room at the time moderating said: 'He's bleeding from somewhere else. This isn't an electrical fault with his heart, his heart doesn't have enough blood to keep pumping.'

That's when they opened my chest up and at the same time another surgeon opened my stomach and it was full of blood as my spleen had burst. My guts are awash with blood. One geezer is trying to stop the bleeding from my spleen, and another is trying to start my heart. Bloody optimists.

At one point I had ten pairs of hands in my body.

The Tube hand-hold pole went through my spleen and lacerated my liver and punctured one of my kidneys. I had a ruptured colon, a ruptured bowel, broken ribs, two punctured lungs, a punctured kidney, burst spleen and a lacerated liver. I lost an eye, an eardrum totally blown out one side, perforated on the other.

I had 42 stitches in my mouth where the blast ripped out pieces of flesh. I had 160 or so stitches around random bits of my body, 104 stitches in my chest and 27 staples in my stomach, 198 stitches holding the left stump together. They didn't close the right one. They amputated below the knee where the injury was but that got infected and I was likely to die, so they amputated through the knee.

They left that wound open to try and aerate it and drain all the infection out of it. They opened the back of the upper leg and took my hamstring out because they thought it was infected. I've got a scar that's the full length of the back of my leg.

The doctors cashed in. Embedded in my body they found and removed £7.40 in one pound coins and ten and 20 pence pieces. And my door keys. And left some of the loose change, the 20 pence piece still lodged in my thigh bone.

There's a wound on the back of my head, the tracheostomy [surgery into the windpipe], the cannulas [tubes in the vein] everywhere, have left their marks. There's not a part of me that ain't been cut open, stitched up or manhandled. The burns aren't too bad, they healed up pretty well.

The bomb made a terrible mess.

I can't associate me today with the photographs of how I was when they stretchered me into St Mary's Hospital. When I look at the photographs of my immediate post-blast body, I can't believe it's me. After eight weeks, I was moved into intensive care, and I could see that disbelief reflected in the eyes of everyone caring for me. How could a human being suffer *that* and survive?

When they thought I was able to take in how much of me was ripped to bits, my consultant, Dr Richard Lyons, explained my injuries.

I shrugged. I knew my legs were gone from being in the tunnel. I looked at him and said: 'Am I going to die? Tell me if I'm going to die?'

He was honest. He said to me, 'You are far from out of the woods yet, we don't know what's going to happen.' He kept looking me in the eye and promised: 'We will do everything we can to prevent that from happening.'

My dad was squeezing my hand. The doctor, Richard, was lovely, he really was, and it was one of the few times that I really welled up. But I didn't cry. With the medical staff, to their fantastic credit, their take on it was that I'd fought so hard to make it to hospital that no matter what, they were going to keep me alive. I wouldn't blame them if they'd looked away and thought it might be kinder to let me fade out. Put their hands up in surrender. After dying twice, it took quite a long time to start the heart manually and they expected if I didn't die that day, I'd die very, very soon. I grasped on to anything, and black humour was easiest.

Andy Harper was the anaesthetist when they first brought me in . They were doing some procedure and I was screaming and shouting, out of it, and yelling: 'Don't bring fucking needles, I don't do fucking needles.' Then, he stuck me. When he came around later, I told him: 'You're the guy who killed me first time round.'

The messing about with the medics helped me in recovery, gave me a life connection, but that commitment from Andy and all the medics for me not to die that day was unreal.

I had 70 operations in about eight weeks. My dad said in one 24-hour period they saw me for five minutes and the rest of the time I was in an operating theatre. The docs would repair something and then something else would go wrong, my lungs would fill with blood and need to be drained. I've always been a big bloke and carried a bit more weight than I should have but I've always been naturally very strong. I played football, did weight training, and boxed. I kept myself in pretty good shape. I liked to have a beer and eat burgers and stuff like that, as most young men do, but being strong the doctors reckon that my sheer body mass, the bulk of me, was what saved me. When the blast attacked, my muscles absorbed it.

My dad said that when they first saw me in the intensive care unit, I had a big bandage running down the front where they'd opened my stomach up, and on either side of it and on my arms and all over me, was like a deep purple, what they call a *plasma bruise*. The shock wave of the blast congealed my blood and that discolours the skin, comes to the surface like jelly. My dad said I was a crimson colour for about six weeks where I'd taken the full shock wave of the blast.

About three or four weeks into the coma, my kidneys started to fail and then completely packed up. They put me on a dialysis machine for two weeks but didn't think they'd start again. They tested my brother for a match and asked him if they needed could they rip one of his out and give it to me. He was happy with that, but luckily my kidney function kicked in. Next, my liver packed up. Every time I took a step forward, I'd take two back, but starting from dead we were gradually getting to moving forward to where they thought I might not cark it. I managed to breathe for 24 hours without the help of a ventilator on 13 August. The guillotine was stuck. For the moment. But hovering.

THE VIEW FROM THE LIFESAVERS

Graeme Baker, a paramedic with the London Ambulance Service said: 'We found Dan half under the train, half out. I decided to stay with him because of his injuries. I tried to reassure him that help was on the way.

'Once supplies got down there, I gave him shots of pain-killers straight into the arm, and we were able to set up a drip to give fluids. I managed to get him out of the station and into an ambulance, with the help of firemen. He was in a fair bit of pain, but he was conscious. He managed to tell me his name, which I thought was a good sign. It was only a mile to St Mary's, but the streets were chaotic. I went with Dan straight into the casualty department, which had been put on standby 40 minutes earlier. There were five resuscitation teams set up in separate bays, waiting, full of nervous energy, to receive the first patients.'

Marcelle Tauber, a senior respiratory nurse who was sent into the A&E to provide extra help, saw Dan arrive: 'I won't ever forget the sight of this paramedic, covered head to foot in soot and dust, running in with him.

'The paramedic was sweating profusely, but I thought he was very controlled at the same time, telling us what drugs and fluids he'd given the patient. Dan was able to talk at this stage but was confused. He told me he was an asthmatic, and that lying down wasn't good for him. Then he said, "I need to get to work, why can't I go to work?" I was asked to pick up his left leg to move him. I put my hand under it, and to my astonishment it felt like ribbons. The leg was completely shredded.'

After he was sedated, Dan deteriorated quickly. His right leg was still attached to the knee, but the foot was turned 180 degrees in the wrong direction. His left eye was very badly damaged, and he had burns across his arms. He had sustained a large cut across the forehead. One eardrum was perforated. Minutes after arriving, he had a cardiac arrest and David Toresen, a senior resuscitation officer, recalled: 'The atmosphere was strangely calm, because everyone knew what they were supposed to do. Calm spreads, in the same way that panic does.'

Professor Nick Peters added: 'Technically, Dan had died, and we brought him back to life.'

Back with the living, he was taken upstairs for a full CT (computed tomography scan) to see what damage had been done to his head and torso.

Caroline Green, the senior radiographer on duty said: 'It was a complete shock when he came in, because not one of us had ever seen anyone in this state before. The scan itself took ten minutes but moving him was difficult and afterwards it took eight of us to clean away the blood, the soot and the debris from where he had been on the scanner.

'A lot of us cried when we got home that evening. The enormity of what he had been through – and what others had been through – just sank in. I had no idea whether any human being could survive such injuries.'

In the operating theatre, the South African vascular surgeon Duncan Black, a veteran of trauma surgery, was in charge of a team fearful of what they might find: 'Dan had very severe injuries to both lower limbs, as well as to the left eye, his head and his arms. There were secondary burns over the arms and the face. He was losing blood fast – faster than we could replace it.'

Four surgeons treated Dan at the same time and present were three theatre sisters, scrub nurses, an anaesthetist, and a cardiothoracic registrar. Behind them stood a range of staff who were asked to provide equipment as it was needed.

Duncan Black said he could see that neither of Dan's legs was salvageable: 'They were very badly damaged, and the flesh had died. If that flesh is not removed, then it can cause contamination and lead to sepsis [blood poisoning].'

A remarkable set of procedures started. Duncan Black began removing the left leg, which had been destroyed right up to the hip bone. Another surgeon, Ragheed Al Mufti, started to remove his right leg below the knee. As they began to operate, Dan's pulse vanished off the screen – another major cardiac arrest and the team had moments to find what was wrong. Their attempts to restart the heart using external resuscitation and defibrillation failed, and, as a last hope, they tried internal cardiac massage, where a doctor has to hold the heart and squeeze it until the blood begins to flow through it.

Black cut open the chest and a cardiothoracic registrar, Jo Chikwe, put her hand inside Dan's ribcage and gently squeezed the muscle.

Chikwe could feel that it was empty, no blood was going through it: so although they had the bleeding from the legs under control, he must be losing blood from somewhere else. To find the source of bleeding, they cut him open down the middle of the torso.

General surgeon Dimitri Hadjiminas discovered Danny's spleen had burst. He removed the spleen and the bleeding was controlled. The surgeons carried on with the double amputation and Dan was cleaned up. His burns were treated, and they examined the left eye, which had been badly damaged by flying debris. They found the loose money and his bunch of keys embedded into his right leg. One 20 pence piece was too deeply embedded to risk it being taken out.

One of the scrub nurses, Natalie Domantaye, said: 'We were physically shattered afterwards, and I think we were doubtful he could survive. But we'd done the best we could.'

The many pints of blood pumped into Dan were the work of a team of haematologists who spent much of that day in casualty carrying around a cool bag full of Group O rhesus negative blood, a blood group which can be safely used on any patient. Dan's body was greedy for it. He went into intensive care looking like a grotesque drawing, his face swollen to three times normal.

Irish nurse Theresa O'Flaherty spent many nights sitting

with him and holding his hand: 'We thought he was a 55-year-old man because the explosion had aged him in some way. For the first few days it was taking it hour by hour, seeing if he had the strength to pull through.' Emergency surgery didn't cure everything.

On 11 July, Dan got a condition known as Sirs, sudden inflammatory response syndrome, where the body turns upon itself and produces toxins, as a result of the bruising and the damage from the blast, that can bring on kidney failure. He had also picked up an infection lying on the rail tracks. A fungus, which can kill, grows on the walls of the London Underground and had infected his lungs but microbiologist Dr Annette Jepson identified and treated it.

Seven days after the first operation, Dan underwent another within the intensive care unit, to remove his damaged left eye. Colin Haylock, a specialist from the Charing Cross Hospital, made a false eye which moves around the eye socket. It's hard to tell that it is a prosthetic eye. He had three more operations to repair different parts of his body and prevent infections.

Intensive care consultant Dr Simon Ashworth said: 'You could see this willpower coming through as we dealt with one problem after another, but everyone gave a little extra for him. I think people quietly felt that to make Danny better was, in a small way, an act of defiance against terrorism. After all, nothing else stands so clearly against the ethos of any hospital.'

No longer sedated, Dan wrote messages to the doctors

and nurses on a blackboard. He couldn't talk after his tracheostomy, where a hole is made through the throat to the windpipe to open the airway. It was often uneasy communication for all involved. Dan was in torment most nights, flashbacks and nightmares, and would hear the screams of people who died next to him.

Nurse Noreen McHale said: 'We would tell him where he was, and that he was safe, but I remember him writing on his board: "You don't see the things I see when I close my eyes". I didn't know what to reply.'

****

My questions and hallucinatory problems began when I opened my eyes in the intensive care ward of St Mary's and I was alive. I could hear noises. Where was I? I was 'safe' in a hospital bed, but could I ever truly escape the tunnel? No matter the sedatives and medication, the mental anguish flourished.

In my head I was at war with myself. The impact of the attack, the aftermath on all our lives, on those closest to me was fractious. There are people who don't appear in this book, not because I don't care for them, but rather to prevent more hurt. In their way, they had much to cope with. I, for once in the true sense of the word, was literally a changed man.

As my body began healing, my mind went into turmoil. The hospital bed. The silence of the night and the sounds, subliminal warnings of mortality that echoed, no matter how deep the coma. Now, I heard them in real time. One of the starkest memories is when I came out of the coma. My dad was at my bedside, I'd had the tracheostomy and couldn't talk. I was trying to write notes. My handwriting is rubbish at the best of times but then I was all over the page courtesy of being paralysed and bunged up with drugs for nine weeks. I scribbled:

'Did it make the news?'

My dad gave me a look that said: *are you kidding me?*

He told me that it wasn't just the train I was on but there were other attacks. The enormity slowly worked its way through the fog of drugs. And how long I'd been out of it.

The UK Foreign Secretary Robin Cook had died [6 August 2005] and the former Northern Ireland Secretary Mo Mowlam [19 August 2005] was gone from a brain tumour. I was wondering how long I'd been asleep.

When I first opened my eyes, kind of sleepwalking out of the coma, I thought it was 7 July 2005, that Thursday morning. I couldn't process how my mum and dad were there, and my brother from New York. I was looking at these people thinking, how have you got here so quickly? And they all looked really orange. My retinas were burned and because of the drops being put in my eyes I saw them as deep, deep orange. I thought: *You bastards, you've been on holiday without me. How dare you.*

I've got this beard, bit of a Rip Van Winkle as it turns out. But they're – *they're orange*. It was insane, like the hallucinations I was having because of all the drugs being pumped into me.

Anybody that takes ketamine recreationally, they're much braver than me, because I was on loads of that stuff as an anaesthetic and it's evil. I did not enjoy that one little bit. It's an extraordinary thing, your life is suddenly paused and the world goes on. That's hard to deal with. How can they be living normally when I'm here fighting to survive?

That was always difficult for me having a two-month block where I've got no concept of what went on in the world. I couldn't tell you, for love nor money, what went on. But one of the things that irritated me, once I'd got out of intensive care and onto a normal hospital ward, was listening to politicians talking around 7/7 and the British bulldog spirit and all that. Bollocks. People were using the Tube and going to work because they've got families to support and mortgages to pay. It was necessity. Nothing more.

It was like trying to ramp up the Blitz spirit. My granddad was in the RAF during the Second World War. The Blitz spirit? He said everyone was fucking terrified. It wasn't like, oh, let's all have a singsong in the Underground. He said it was people crying and screaming and in genuine fear.

Political claptrap diminishes, I think, the reality of what happens. They waffle on about being an island nation which can take it all and dish it out, but most of them are never going to experience real life. It's the grunts, the rest of us, who must use public transport and take the risk every day. I'll never not be angry about their attitude.

I spent much of my weeks in intensive care in the valley

of the 'dolls', on a course of Valium to ease my panic attacks. The flashbacks were incessant and seemed to accelerate the more I healed and was discharged from intensive care into the Zachary Cope ward. This was like the TV show *The Twilight Zone*; strange and frightening manifestations began. I wanted to shut out the world. I couldn't bear to see others or to hear others. There was a wonderful Sister on the ward, Naj el Mahi, and she helped me. She and the other nurses were good at boosting my confidence, but it was in the night that I truly needed them. I'd wake up screaming '*fire, fire!*' – convinced that everyone around me was going to be engulfed in flames.

Many times, I warned the nurses, screaming and shouting, that there was a bomb on the train. Naj el Mahi said: 'When Danny arrived, he was very depressed and withdrawn. Very often, at 3am, one of us would be with him after he had had some terrible dream. We couldn't take the dreams away, but we could be there to reassure him that everything was OK.'

I see the irony that one of the most soothing of all my carers, a person who truly helped me in the early days of what I learned was Complex Post Traumatic Stress Disorder (CPTSD), was Sister Naj, a cheerful Muslim nurse, the best of the best, who seemed to be there every time I needed attention, from a glass of water to a soothing jab up the arse. And I required plenty of them.

One witching hour, at 3am in the Zachary Cope, I was lying on top of the bed sheet on the perfectly made hospital bed and watching a video of the telly series *Red Cap*. That did it. Nothing to do with the lovely star of it, Tamzin Outhwaite, but that was the moment my emotional dam burst. My mind played with me: *This bed looks so big because I'm taking up such a small part of it.*

I'm sitting up, so even more this bed looks like an enormous ocean in front of me, and I burst out crying. I thought of how ten weeks before, I'd have filled out the whole fucking bed. Now, I don't even take up half of it. And it was real and the magnitude of it all hit me like a sledge-hammer. Who is going to want me after this? How can I work? What and when and FUCK! I broke. The nurses came over and they were going to sedate me if I didn't calm down because I'm waking up the other patients, I was in a terrible state. Sister Naj was there, calm and in control and helping.

Suddenly I stopped crying, being so upset. I thought: *That's it – don't do that again.* And I didn't cry at all for eight years. I put it out there and it stayed there. If I get upset, I become angry, and the anger overtakes the sadness and I physically can't cry. I feel my eyes go but the anger kicks in and I think: *Damn that fucking animal Khan for doing this* and that emotion takes over. It took and takes some doing.

I come from a tough East End of London family and was brought up with the diktat that men don't cry – whatever it takes you to get through it without looking weak. No matter, that's what you do. That was ingrained into me from a young age

Khan truly fucked me up physically and mentally. I went from 6ft 4in tall to five foot-nothing. Oh, yes, I hate him, and I still feel anger toward him. I have no anger or distaste about Muslims or their religion. But I despise Khan.

Never more than when he intrudes on my life. He can appear at any time and take me back to the tunnel. And I am *there*. I may be sitting at home or in a restaurant or in the car, but I am back in that tunnel. Khan takes me there. As does the poor girl who died in my carriage. I saw her crawling up my hospital bed demanding to know why I didn't help her. Still do see her sometimes.

It's the PTSD and the survivor's guilt. There were people who were killed when their injuries weren't as bad as mine. Why me? Why did I survive and somebody else didn't? Why did I survive when I was watching people die around me and I couldn't do anything to help them? So many people have told me they should have been on that train that morning but one of the kids was ill, or they went home to collect some forgotten paperwork. Happenings in a split second, which can change the course of your life.

Forget logic and reason. There's a part of your brain which can't compute that. A terrorist attack is such an irrational act it is something that your mind can't process, that somebody would set out to do this. But then when you try to match irrational and logical the two don't go together and the brain warps. Everybody tells me not to feel guilty, it's not your fault. I know, but when you're told constantly by medical people you shouldn't have survived, you get in a spin. Is there more valour in death?

As I drifted between life and death, the world outside the walls of St Mary's was furiously agonising about and investigating 7/7. I found it difficult to take in too much of the information, I spent hours torturing myself – was I a coward, crying and screaming and being saved by Adrian? Why couldn't I save myself? Was the constant beating myself up why I couldn't save anyone else? Ridiculous, of course, but that was exactly what my frame of mind was – ridiculous. There's no reason why that person next to me died and I didn't; you have to just thank your lucky stars that you survived and move forward with it.

But survivor's guilt is incredibly difficult to live with. It would really affect me when I would meet a family member of somebody who was killed on the train I was on. It would absolutely break me because I was looking at somebody who's in absolute pain having lost a loved one and I'm sitting there thinking Khan was sitting right next to me, yet here I am. In trying to make sense of it you drive yourself inside out.

I feel that mental torture was, and can be, as agonising as being blown in bits out of that Tube carriage. In those first awake hospital days I had a 50-50 chance of survival but out of the coma it was 100 percent certain Khan, the ringleader of the bombers, would show up on the ward. And the cruelly injured girl crawling ever so slowly towards me on many, many nights. I'd love to properly convey the terror of that but unless you've been there, and many people have for a myriad of reasons, it's other-worldly and there is no handbook.

It was only when I got out of hospital that I grasped the reality of what my situation was, how ill-equipped the world was and is for somebody with a disability and learning to come to terms with PTSD, survivor's guilt and trying to process that someone tried to murder me. I'm not just a survivor, I'm a survivor of an attempted murder, and that's quite a powerful thing to know yourself. I stood next to somebody that hated me and everybody else on that carriage and wanted to kill us all. That is a huge driving force for me saying: *You do not win.*

I want to set an example for the next person who is involved in an incident like I was, or someone who has a catastrophic car accident, to say, this isn't the end of your life, it's the end of a chapter. And now it's a new chapter. And I'm very, very lucky in so many respects. I'm very lucky to have survived, and I'm also very lucky in a way that will surprise you: I got to wipe the slate clean. I got to build a new life for myself from scratch. And to see how that works out, we'll have to wait, I've only been at it for 20 years. I still had the choices to decide what I wanted to do and build my life.

I don't have any photos of me prior to the attack because I had to say goodbye to the person that I was on the morning of 7 July and try to reinvent myself to be the person I am now. There was no point hankering for things that would never be again – I will never walk again, I will never run, I'll never play football again. Life isn't going to give me another kick of the ball. The whole essence of who I was, a tall, tough footballer and boxer, was gone. I don't see the point in looking at something that I'm not anymore, I'm not that person, I'll never be that again. I needed to start afresh. But that doesn't mean my brain stops telling me to get up and walk.

Every day my body is craving to stand up. Oh, I tried and tried and was encouraged to do so by Dr Richard Lyons. He helped get me a referral to the amputee ward at the Douglas Bader Rehabilitation Centre at Queen Mary's Hospital in Roehampton in London. If you're going to get back on your feet, these are the people to do it.

The centre, so new in 2006 I could smell the paint, was named after the World War Two fighter pilot, a famous ace despite having lost his legs in a 1931 aerobic display accident. He was immortalised by Kenneth More in that so very British, so very stiff-upper-lip, 1956 film, *Reach for the Sky*. Clever science – aka 'tin legs' – enabled Douglas Bader to build the life he wanted, and I hoped this eponymous facility would give me that chance.

Dr Lyons came to see me before I went there. Now, remember this is only a few weeks since he stood by my bed and said he thought I'd die. This time he's telling me something life enhancing – and, to me, what will always be remarkable. He said that during the First World War his great-grandfather was at the 1916 Battle of the Somme, five months of fighting, which included the deadliest day in British military history, and how his great-grandfather, like tens of thousands of others, was really badly injured. Nevertheless, he carried on in the trenches and for his bravery received a military medal. Dr Lyons told me: 'For most of my life I looked at that man as the bravest man I ever met but not now. I don't know how you've done it because I don't know how you're getting through it.'

There was a moment then when I almost broke my rule about turning to tears, but I didn't succumb. I determined even more to crack on, which I did, but not without difficulty.

Chapter Four

GONNA FLY NOW

'Money talks, but it don't sing and dance and it don't walk.'
– NEIL DIAMOND, FOREVER IN BLUE JEANS,
(NEIL DIAMOND, RICHARD BENNETT), 1979

'I'VE BEEN BLOWN UP – not touched up!'

I told that to the psychologist, a specialist in sexual trauma, because she didn't seem to know the difference.

I'd happily accepted counselling as I wasn't coping well with being told I'd spend the rest of my life in a wheelchair. The doctors decided my level of injuries were too severe for prosthetic legs. I couldn't accept that then.

Even today, sometimes when I wake up, I yearn to go for a run.

Imagine what my body and brain were dictating to me in those first days without my legs. I wanted to sprint. But the mind doctors weren't much use in dealing with my cravings – and my rather obvious limitations. I didn't have any psychological support.

My first trauma counsellor seemed nice enough. I thought I wouldn't bore him with the details of the tunnel and only gave him a general idea of what happened to me. When I'd finished running through the PTS nightmares, he sat back in his chair, took a few deep breaths, and said: 'I need to leave the room and get some water.'

I never saw him again. The medical staff said my experience was too much for this psychiatrist. I thought: *If he's a professional and he can't cope what are the chances of me being able to deal with it? He's the one supposed to give me the mechanisms to cope.*

Most nights I'd see the girl that died being disgusted at me and pleading for help. Khan became a shadow dancing around my brain and on the walls of the hospital ward. I'd feel I was on fire, ablaze, on the tunnel floor, waiting to die, and then Khan – not an apparition in my brain – was trying to get at me or lying on the bed looking at me. The terror was I felt I could touch him. I could touch him, but not stop him. I saw dead faces and had that panic, for they had no right to be there. It was illicit. They were dead. The provenance for all this was the horror. Of 7/7, and the present.

I craved help and I was assigned a blind therapist who specialised in trauma brought on by sexual incidents. No matter how much I explained about the tunnel and my nightmares and hallucinations she kept coming around to issues about childhood and sex and that's when I lost it and told her I'd been blown up and not sexually assaulted. I was so disenchanted with the sessions – it was only another box being ticked – that I used to spend the time playing games on a PlayStation my brother had given me. I'd have Arsenal on the screen playing in some big game and the only sound was a *click click* as I controlled the screen and got immersed in the action.

The therapist was chatter, chatter, gobbledegook to me, as I passed the time. It all went wrong when I forgot the situation and when I lost a game I screamed: 'Bollocks.' The therapist twigged and I confessed what had been going on and she was distraught. I found I was counselling her.

I recognise how angry I was at Roehampton. Furious at what had happened but frustrated, so fucking frustrated, at what I could not do – and could not have. I couldn't have real legs, and I kept being told prosthetic legs weren't for me. Roehampton wouldn't accept me at first; they said I had to go to Charing Cross Hospital in London but that's not a rehabilitation unit, it's a normal hospital with a pros-thetics department. It upset me that I'd had to fight to get into Roehampton to get treated.

Didn't I have enough battles? Someone decides what you are and how you'll be treated and it's not easy to get out of that box. It's ticked. You're in it. And all the time I suffer excruciating phantom leg pain. My parents were told if I survived, I would never walk, I'd be in a wheelchair for life. Roehampton said it wouldn't be worth it, but I asked: 'Let me try.' I couldn't let go without going for it, never mind the pain, the mental and physical agony. I was determined to make my body fit, if you'll excuse the pun, for prosthetic legs. The need to stand up was worth any risk. I did physio two or three times a day when I could. And I'd get pissed off when I couldn't have a session.

What with my PTS and anger and frustrations, I'd get really upset. It seemed to me that others, especially women, were getting all the attention, at my cost. Everyone but me seemed to be in and out with shiny plastic and chrome prosthetic legs.

It was a weird place to be, where it was normal to see people with no arms or legs. And envy them for having artificial ones. My mind was in turmoil, but I so wanted to walk, and I *needed* the opportunity.

My physio Maggie was wonderful. I'd get there at 8.30am but I might not see her until 11.30am because she'd been with others. I seemed to get ten minutes here and there when it suited. It seemed to me that it's always put across that it's much worse for a woman to lose her legs, but it's hard to be a man without legs, believe that. You might imagine how I felt being told: 'Don't bother coming down today, we're going to be tied up.'

It reached a point where my dad turned around and told the doctors: 'I'm not being funny, but my boy is sitting on his arse doing nothing. Others need to do rehab too, but don't ignore my son. He's sitting there watching others walking around and it's not fair.'

They brought in another physio, a Welsh guy called Gareth, and he was brilliant. There were many of us injured that day. The 7/7 rehab had to fit in around particular people's rehab schedule. And that really pissed me off.

I liked everyone, they were nice, but there was a clear disparity in the early days of Roehampton. I have nothing but the utmost respect for the physio staff and the incredibly talented individuals who make the artificial limbs but it seemed to me there were politics involved at times which leaves you in utter despair.

It always felt like a man losing his legs somehow wasn't as bad as a woman losing her legs. Women also attracted attention. I thought if a woman wanted her prosthetic legs painted gold, they'd have done it for them as it would get in the newspapers.

The media did help me, particularly Louisa Preston, a news presenter from the BBC. I'd been asked and did a load of interviews as I recovered at Roehampton and Louisa pitched up. They point blank refused to give me a pair of computerised prosthetic legs, they call them 'C-legs', and on them you can feel as wobbly as a drunken sailor, but neither 'C-legs' or 'sea-legs' was I getting. When Louisa asked me if there was anything she could do, I told her about these new prosthetics that had come out that I wanted to try but wasn't being allowed. She couldn't understand why because she'd had a tour of the facility with the camera crew and seen patients up on the parallel bars and fitted with prosthetics and working with them. But not me.

She said: 'Who is your consultant?'

As she said it, he walked past.

'That's him.'

Quick as a flash, she went over and spoke to him.

Next day, I had legs.

Since then I don't complain about the BBC licence fee.

The legs are around £30,000 – each. I could only have one of the 'C-legs'. That was the left leg sorted. On the right, I had what was called a locked joint leg so there was no articulation in the knee joint so when you sat down you pulled a lever and the leg dropped and bent, and when you stood up you had to flick it into place.

On the left it was all *Star Trek*. It had a computer microprocessor in the knee and another one in the heel of the foot and yet one more in the ball of the foot. To make it safe to walk, it calculated what your body weight was and when you took a step you had to get 70 percent of your body weight transferring to the ball of the prosthetic foot. This then sends a signal to the knee joint and allows the knee to break so it would bend and, as you took a step forward, you had to kick it forward and it would lock it down again, and you get the weight transference. The idea is that once it's locked, if you stumble, it's not going to give way underneath you.

It's a really safe leg to use, the sensor's doing the protecting, and it makes walking much more natural, and I desperately wanted to try it. I felt they were disgruntled that they'd been compelled into it by Louisa from the BBC – they didn't want a negative 7/7 victim's story on the Six O'Clock News – and one arrogant physio told me:

'It won't work for somebody with your level of injury. It won't work.'

I said: 'You're defining me by my injuries. Fuck you.'

I walked up a flight of stairs with my new legs. I got to the top of the stairs.

It was like *Rocky*; I could hear the triumphant theme music. in my head.

I held on to the banister with one hand and waved in the air and shouted: 'Showed you.'

'Yes, it worked but we didn't think it would.'

'You assumed, you didn't know,' I pointed out. 'Everyone assumed I was going to die but here I am.'

I do think being bloody-minded has kept me alive, kept me fighting and somehow surviving my own attempts to destroy myself. Seems I even get bloody-minded at myself, and just as well.

My *Rocky* moment is a fond memory but my experience with trying to walk with prosthetics was not smooth, it involved many stumbles and hurdles. And pain. Specialists, occupational therapists, physiotherapists, taught me how to cope without legs, to keep my balance while sitting up and to strengthen my arms. As I was getting stronger someone said there was always light at the end of the tunnel and I had to laugh telling them: 'Don't talk to me about bloody tunnels, I've seen enough of those.' Sadly, it's not like the movies when they strap on the tin legs and five minutes later the star is doing the four-minute mile. It's not like that at all. I so wanted to walk, to be tall again, to be fully grown again, be myself again, but the pain was and is incredible.

Some of what I'm going to explain may sound crazy, but I've learned how complex, how astonishing, the human body is. You might think you're in charge but that body you spend every day in is the boss. And a bloody dictator. Walking with prosthetic legs is painful and tiring and – this is the crazy bit – I don't get anything out of it. I lose more than I get. It's been stop and start over the years. My body constantly craves to stand up. My brain is nagging: *Stand up, get up.* And, rather obviously, I can't. Which is why I'm a bit of an expert on phantom pain. My brain wants me upright and tells me to stand up and I can't react to that command so the brain assumes my legs must be damaged and sends phantom pain, like an alert, an alarm going off.

The horror is that because I can't react by standing up from that first burst of pain, the brain sends another blast through. And keeps on doing so and I can't take it and I'm screaming and fidgeting. Then you get a lull, the brain must get tired of being ignored, and you get ten minutes of a normal level of pain and then bang! It's back, like a crescendo it builds and builds, drops off, and starts again. It's like that every single day. It's all pain, no gain. When I stand on prosthetic legs all my phantom pain goes because I'm upright in body *and* mind. I look down and I've got feet! I've got cool trainers on. I look in the mirror and there's this tall guy with jogging bottoms on. I'm 'me' again. My brain loves this and so do I. But I can only be 'me' for about ten minutes, because it absolutely kills me. Every time I take the prosthetics off, it's like losing my legs all over again. Imagine, three or four times a day, having that grief of losing your legs.

The legs weren't this big upgrade in my life. It was a reminder of what I couldn't do. I couldn't run. I couldn't kick a ball. I couldn't box. I couldn't do leg presses or ride a bike. I couldn't drive a car the way I'd normally drive a car. The legs weren't a reflection of what I could do now, but a reminder of all the things I couldn't do. It was cosmetic as much as anything. When I sat down again the phantom pain would come back tenfold. The only gain from using the legs is because as humans we're not designed to be sitting down all the time and without legs my internal organs get compacted, and I have problems with taking a pee as all my insides get squished up. I can keep trying to use the legs but emotionally and psychologically, you have to weigh it all up as it might push me back to the deep, deep depths of where I was mentally. There's a cost to being in a wheelchair that I will pay at some point in my life. I know that, and as much as I don't want it, you have to accept that's what it is.

Everything I've ever wanted to do since I left hospital care I've done from my chair. I can walk on the artificial legs but not even to the front door without being drenched in sweat and in excruciating pain. I hadn't stood up or walked for about four years when I went to an amputee clinic and they took measurements and fitted the legs. My muscle memory is so good that the minute they were on my brain knew what to do and I walked up and down the parallel bars, no problem, but my body was screaming at me in pain. I kept pushing myself and that's my problem. I don't walk up and down a little bit and then sit down. I keep on going on – I'm making up for lost time. I'm sweating like it's going out of fashion, I'm bright red but I know the legs must come off at some point, so I'm making the most of it. Ridiculous behaviour.

Especially with me intimately knowing the state of me.

On the left side, I've got as close to a through-hip amputation you can get without going through the hip. I've got a tiny amount of bone left from what was my left thigh and because it was a blast injury and not a disease it's still alive and my body reacts as if my leg is broken and is still releasing calcium. On the X-rays you can see this great big hook that goes to a point and a big cloud of calcified bone. Normally calcification from a blast injury goes quite deep into the soft tissue but mine doesn't, it's about two millimetres from the surface. If I were to misstep, it would rip through the skin.

The other issue is that where the bone hook is closer to my groin I've got an artery there. When the surgeons cut my artery back, it's like elastic, it shot back up into my groin. So, with the wrong movement I could easily get an arterial bleed. There are always choices. I can do this but run the risk of that. And vice versa. I have hernias which come from my time at Roehampton. I'd be walking up the hill and lose my footing and brace myself and the chain reaction involving the internal scars would result in a hernia popping out. I've already got loads. That was the challenge every time I walked.

As much as I'd love to put the prosthetic legs on and walk into work, it can't happen. If I tried it would be carnage, I'd be a big heap on the ground. It's the same as putting them on at home and walking around the house for ten minutes – I'd only feel like shit for the rest of the day, and that's not worth the emotional upset. It is difficult to accept that I'm forever going to be sat down, that my waist-level view of the world is never going to change. I explained that I wake up some mornings and I want to go for a run and that's because I was a sportsman. That part of me didn't get blown out of me. There's a football pitch near where I live and when I drive by, it's still inside me, I think: *If I could only have another 90 minutes of that.*

I miss that today, so many years on, as strongly as when it first happened. To have that sensation again, putting the kit on and a pair of keeper's gloves and standing on a pitch and having the sense of catching a ball, that feeling of it hitting my hands, and reverberating through the arms. I can still remember it and I'll never experience it again. It's another curse of the bombing, my heightened sensitivities.

Every time I drive by these football pitches and see the players I think: *They have no idea how lucky they are.* Every Sunday, and every Saturday and Wednesday night, they're going to be there with their mates having a game or a kick around. I can't, and none of that was my choice. I can't watch 90 minutes of football on the telly. I sit there and I feel the sadness coming out. I can watch the first half and *Match of the Day*, but a full match is too much, and that's 20 years on. That feeling is just as raw now as it was when I was in St Mary's on my bed watching England vs Northern Ireland at Windsor Park in Belfast. I lay there staring through the telly rather than watching because all I could think of was the matches that I'd played in. The real kicker for me was I booked a holiday to see my mum and dad in Spain in April before the July bombings. I played semi-pro football for the Metropolitan Police, but also played Sunday League football and the last game I played for my Romford and Dagenham League team, Interlink Express, was a cup semi-final and we won. We were a new team, and we'd finished third in the league and made it to the final. I couldn't change my flight, and I missed the big match.

I'd had a drink with the team manager Ron and he offered to help pay to change the flight but I explained I simply couldn't. I said I would do him a deal – that next season we'd get through to another final and I'll be there and we'll win. He shook my hand and told me: 'I'll keep you to that.' And then I got blown up. Even with my heart pumping in good order (80 BPM) that was never going to happen. It's little things like that which bring on the horrors. I remember the conversation, sitting there with Ron, and making plans. They say man plans, and God laughs. People say 'it's only football' but that was my life. I worked and played football. That was it. Anybody who knew me understood that: 'He's the goalkeeper.'

Everyone knew me. Because that's what I did. I was the goalkeeper.

'It's only football' remarks were like 'it's only walking'. Football was as much a part of me as standing on two legs. If I wasn't playing, I would be training or in the gym keeping myself fit. The amount of money I spent on goal-keeping gloves. I think I worked to fund my football. That's what it was.

I loved every minute of it. And I've never done anything that comes close to replacing the feeling I got sitting in a dressing room. I had superstitions, and I wouldn't put my right glove on until I was on the penalty spot. I'd walk across the pitch before I put my left glove on.

Every Sunday League football morning going into the local newsagent and buying the same bottle of soda, the same pack of chewing gum, and putting them into the back of the net to have during the game. In ten years, I never changed the drink because I thought if I did, I would have a nightmare of a game. It's stupid, I know, but a thing that you do. When you can never do them again that means the world.

What many people don't get is that it's not simply the walking you can't do that hurts, it's every other aspect of life that goes with it. And that takes some adjusting to. If you think what you did in the last 20 minutes – got out of bed, grabbed a cup or a glass at the top of a cupboard, climbed up the stairs or stood up, stood in the shower, stepped in and out of a bath. It's an endless list. Everything I used to do I can't do now, or I have to do differently. It's not only me, there are nine million disabled people in the UK in 2025, and I'd like people to have some inkling of what life, daily life, is like for us. Tea and toast – even that can be a challenge. I'm not complaining, only seeking understanding. I'm bad enough at that, at behaving myself. I struggle and I'm pig-headed and stubborn – *'I can do it!'* – and sometimes too proud. In my case, pride usually guaranteed a fall.

Chapter Five

MEMENTO MORI

'Someone I once loved gave me a box full of darkness. It
took me years to understand that this, too, was a gift.'
– MARY OLIVER, THE USES OF SORROW, 1987

I TOLD YOU I didn't think this was a miracle story but
many, many people believe that me being alive is up there
with water turning into wine and all the rest. They point to
the circumstances of my almost demise and when I think
back to the day the security heavy mob boys came to see
me it did all sound a touch supernatural.

When I was in the Douglas Bader centre at Roehampton,
the anti-terrorist squad needed to interview me because I was
the only person that survived from the bomb site, from the
epicentre of the blast. If it had been an earthquake, it would
have been an eight on the Richter scale, that's The Big One.

They said they'd brought my personal effects, they'd
managed to locate a lot of things from the tunnel, and had
them in a pile of evidence bags, if I'd like them back.

'Depends on what's left,' I told them.

One said: 'We've got what's left of your laptop bag, the contents of the bag, your wallet; your credit cards have melted so they've been destroyed. I've got you your rings and I've got your watch. I've got your clothes. Do you want the clothes back?'

I asked him what state the clothes were in. Now, I'm feeling a touch fragile at this time, it's only early days at Roehampton. He said: 'They're bad, covered in blood and God knows what, and they don't smell too good either. I'm happy to dispose of those through our forensics unit but some people have wanted everything back.'

I was happy for them to go but wanted my personal effects. He handed me back the Tumi wallet my brother had given me, its Nubuck leather a light suede colour, and it was crimson with saturated blood. When I started to open it he said to be careful because I'd be shocked by it.

My bank cards had melted and gone but my travel card from the day of the bomb was there, and it was in pristine condition. There's not a fleck of blood on it. There's not a bit of soot on it. Or dust or hair or anything. Pristine, dated: 07.JLY.05. Immaculate. If you went out and bought a travel card today and compared it, you'd think I'd bought mine at the same time, not one that went through a bombing more than two decades ago. Other than the price.

Yet, my wallet on both sides has got these big dark crimson patches where all the blood bled from where my leg was, through my jeans, and onto it. The travel card is not marked one bit – and the credit cards in front of and behind are melted. But it's pristine. Thinking about it brings the chills. When I opened the wallet and saw it, I threw it back on the bed. It freaked me out because it didn't seem possible. Romford Station, the date, the zones, 1-6, it was all as clear as that day.

'Is that my card? You're fucking me about?'

'That's the card you were carrying that day. I've had a full forensics team look at your wallet and we cannot explain why that travel card wasn't burnt to a crisp. When we took out the credit card behind it and your company ID card in front of it, they were brittle and as we took them out they shattered. That card was between them. It's like new.'

They were as puzzled as me, if not as freaked. I was wearing a pair of Oakley glasses – I've worn prescription specs since I was 18 years old – and my glasses case was a solid stainless-steel tube and the pressure of the blast completely crushed it into a matchbox size. I've got bits of my laptop. My bag was all ripped. My notebook was burned and covered in blood and all sorts. I got my watch back. Remember, because I was ablaze the metal strap of my watch burned into my wrist, and I pulled it off.

I've got the imprint of the white star emblem from that watch in my arm. I put my fingernails underneath it to pull it out of my arm to and take it off –and I looked at the time, of all fucking things – and I just threw it onto the track. Just kind of tossed it to one side. When the police gave it back to me the Sekonda watch was still working. They'd cleaned it up but when I opened the clasp, underneath was all my dried blood. They had the gold ring I had on. They said when they cut it off me what was left was like a solid clump and they had it in a petri dish of acid for three weeks trying to dissolve the blood, it was so embedded with dirt and my blood.

The forensics guys told me that when they were working on my stuff one of the staff asked: 'What victim are we putting this down to?'

'He's still alive.'

'There's no fucking way this guy's still alive, no way.'

'Seriously, this belongs to Mr Daniel Biddle, and he is still alive.'

They couldn't get their heads around what had been done to my stuff, considering the amount of pressure and the impact of the blast which they could gauge from the damage to other items they were recovering from the tunnel. There was no way, they said, I should be alive. One of the cops assigned to me had to ring his guvnor up and tell him what was going on and was told: 'I thought you'd be back on the job by now, I thought he'd be dead.'

My guy told him: 'Seriously, if you was to see the state of him when they brought him in. How he's alive I have no fucking idea.'

He said he'd seen people a lot less injured than me who had died. The doctors told me I did look rough. They guessed my age when I first went in and added nearly 30 years. My injuries were more catastrophic than about 80 percent of people that died and that's surreal. I don't know why I'm still here. I took the brunt of it. Khan killed everyone around me. And I was the closest one to him. And people that were standing behind me and had the Perspex screen *and* my bulk between me and them, they died, and I didn't. I don't know how; nobody will ever know.

What I did learn with the help of the anti-terrorist boys and all the other agencies and investigators who came into my life was about the bombers and in the years since, I have found out so much more. My thinking is that as I see Khan rather too often, I should know as much about him as possible. I thought it might help me fight him off and with the nightmares, but I can't say it has for I don't believe that most of us will ever understand what motivates such evil. The Devil wears many guises.

At a longish glance, and that's all I had of him, Mohammad Sidique Khan was a normal-looking bloke, another passenger on the train. I want to remember that maybe he had a vulpine look, an edge about him, a danger sign, but he didn't. He looked normal and that's even more terrifying. I found out he liked to be called Khan, my shorthand name for him; it made him more like one of the lads.

What I gathered about Khan, and his fellow bombers, sounds like a police report and I suppose that's what it most resembles because what I got were facts, not reasons, not explanations, no answers to why so many people had to die and so many had to suffer. For what? When he set off the bomb he was married with a one-year-old child. He'd been a primary school teaching assistant and youth worker who had turned into a suicide bomber. Why? And he was the boss of it all. It is so far beyond my comprehension.

He was born in Leeds on 20 October 1974, the son of Pakistani immigrants who'd become British citizens. The youngest of six children, he grew up in Beeston, a deprived, ethnically mixed area of the city. He went to school locally and his mates from those days said he was a wild lad and into drinking and drugs, accused of being too *Westernised*. It was then he christened himself Khan.

After school, he worked in low-level Government clerical jobs before going to Leeds Metropolitan University in 1996 where he got a second-class business degree. It was at university that he met Hasina, a British Muslim of Indian origin. Their families didn't like the idea, but they married on 2 October 2001 and their daughter was born in May 2004. After his marriage he moved out of Beeston to nearby Batley, and then to Dewsbury, but stayed part of the local scene through his teaching and youth work. My mind boggled when I learned that at the school, he was a 'learning mentor', he helped kids struggling in class – and those with *behavioural problems*. One report I read said of him: 'He was highly regarded by both teachers and parents, showing a real talent for encouraging difficult children, many of whom viewed him as a role model.'

They also reported that he was serious about his Islamic faith and prayed regularly at school and attended the local mosque on Fridays. He told anyone who listened that he had turned to religion after being drawn into gang-style behaviour and using alcohol.

He showed no signs of being a mad bomber – well, maybe. When the anti-terror people started digging into Khan's other life there appeared to be a change of character, more insular, introverted they said, and the regular guy with easy-going manners faded away. He was reported to have been disgruntled, intolerant. He went on a Muslim pilgrimage, a Hajj visit, to Mecca with his wife in 2003. All this time his life, outside his family, revolved around the mosques and Islamic groups of Leeds, Huddersfield and Dewsbury; he worked with Muslim youths, arranging camping and white-water rafting trips. The man with a strong Yorkshire accent was 'a hero' to these kids.

'Kids' like his fellow bombers, Shehzad Tanweer and Hasib Hussain. Khan spent much time with them before they blew me and the rest of us up on 7/7. I'll never know for certain if he was full-time recruiting for extreme Islamism but if I was on a jury the circumstantial evidence would convince me of his guilt. The clincher is that in 2004 he was sacked from his school job after failing to turn up for class and taking weeks and weeks of 'sick leave'. Now, it gets very dark. That year he went to Pakistan with Shehzad Tanweer and our spies, MI5, said – belatedly – that there was contact with members of Osama Bin Laden's al-Qaeda network and weeks spent at a terrorist training camp. And then Khan and fellow bomber Hasib Hussain were on the periphery of another terrorist plot before 7/7.

They were 'monitored' on four separate occasions in February and March 2004 because of associations with a group planning to build a giant fertiliser bomb. Khan 'met' this terror gang through a jihadi network linking the UK, America, and Pakistan. How much MI5 knew about Khan and his cohorts by the morning I struggled off to work and rushed to catch that Tube remains unclear to me. They knew he kept up his Pakistan terror links after he got back to Yorkshire but... but, there's a big *but*.

Apparently, the two of them – Khan and Hasib – were not rated as 'essential' security risks because there was no intelligence they were planning an outrage. Khan was thought to be involved in fraud and wasn't identified but only 'watched'; anti-terrorism officers seemingly focused on other suspects.

When the blokes involved in the fertiliser bomb plot were arrested one of them, Mohammed Junaid Babar, said he was at the same training camp as Khan in Pakistan and recognised his photograph on the telly after we were blown up.

In June 2006, computer expert Martin Gilbertson claimed he had warned West Yorkshire police about the extremist views of Khan and Tanweer when he worked at an Islamic bookshop in Beeston. The police said they had no record of any letter from him. After his death a video surfaced of Khan proclaiming himself a 'soldier' at war against the West. He found willing recruits close to home.

I believe every action Khan took was coolly calculated,

totally premeditated. He chose those who would, without question, carry out the mission. Shehzad Tanweer was born in Bradford in 1987 but lived most of his life in the Beeston area of Leeds, about half a mile from his friend the bus bomber Hasib Hussain. In 2004 he was arrested for wild behaviour and charged with disorderly conduct. That same year he and Khan went to Karachi and the Pakistani authorities confirmed he'd also been there in 2003 when he went to Lahore and Faisalabad and attended a *Madrassa*, an Islamic school.

Tanweer, like Khan, was known to our spooks and met members of the al-Qaeda-linked and outlawed outfit Jaish-e-Muhammad in the months before 7/7. But I found an official report which said: 'There were more pressing priorities at that time including the need to disrupt known plans to attack the UK. It was decided not to investigate them further or seek to identify them.'

Tanweer's uncle, Tahir Pervez, said his nephew and Khan were in Pakistan for many weeks before they returned to Britain in February 2005 and then 'they used to be up all the night talking to each other'.

Tanweer's DNA, along with that of two other suicide bombers, was found at their bomb factory at 18 Alexandra Grove in Leeds, which the police investigated on 12 July 2005. The equipment they'd used to make the bombs to blow us up remained in place. The chemicals they'd used had bleached the bombers' hair – they told their families it was too much chlorine in the municipal swimming pool –

and their minds had been bent by local extremist indoctrination, and during visits to Pakistan and Afghanistan. The how and why of any of that doesn't appear in any official reports. Instead, families were quoted in the archive papers I studied as saying what a nice Yorkshire lad Shehzad Tanweer was. An uncle said: 'He was proud to be British.'

Yet, Shehzad Tanweer detonated a bomb on a London Underground Circle line train between Aldgate and Liverpool Street stations, killing himself and seven people, and injuring more than 100. Maybe somewhere in eternity there is an answer to my everlasting question of why.

A question I repeat again when it comes to Germaine Lindsay. He was born in 1985 in Jamaica but moved a year later with his mother to Huddersfield, West Yorkshire, where in later life he connected with Khan. His father remained in Jamaica and his mother had a new partner who became a tough stepfather to him.

By 1990, he had a new and much kinder stepfather who was around until 2000 when he and his mother converted to Islam. At school he graduated from music and art to kickboxing and was disciplined for distributing al-Qaeda leaflets. He quickly became fluent in Arabic and could quote the Koran at length. His mentor was the Jamaican hate preacher Abdallah al-Faisal, who campaigned for the murder of 'Jews, Americans, Hindus, and Christians and other unbelievers' before being jailed in 2003 and deported from the UK in 2007.

I give you these details because I believe it's important

to know what can go on anywhere in plain sight. You can't simply shrug off what appears as daft ranting and raving. With all that shouting in his ear, Germaine's mum went off to America leaving him home alone in Huddersfield. He quit school and lived on benefits and selling mobile phones and Islamic books. If he fell in love with Islam, he fell even more into it with Samantha Lewthwaite, a white woman whom he met on the internet and later, in person, at a *Stop the War* march in London.

Two years older than him, she was born on 5 December 1983 in Banbridge, County Down, Northern Ireland. Her parents separated in 1994 and when she was 17 years old she converted to Islam, taking the name Sherafiyah.

They married, using the Islamic names Asmantara and Jamal, on 30 March 2002 in Aylesbury, Buckinghamshire, near her family's home. Her parents did not attend the ceremony, unable to accept their daughter's conversion to Islam. They lived in Huddersfield, mixing with Khan and his associates, but moved full-time to Aylesbury in September 2003; six months later their first child was born. Germaine worked as a carpet-fitter, a job he got through his innocent brother-in-law who thought he was a good bloke. Lindsay boarded a Piccadilly line Underground train at King's Cross and detonated a bomb, killing himself and 26 others and injuring more than 340. I can go on asking into eternity, but I doubt I'll get an answer to why. His widow issued a statement:

'I totally condemn and am horrified by the atrocities. I am the wife of Germaine Lindsay, and never predicted or imagined that he was involved in such horrific activities. He was a loving husband and father. I am trying to come to terms with the recent events. My whole world has fallen apart, and my thoughts are with the families of the victims of this incomprehensible devastation.'

She went on to have their second child, and become one of the world's most wanted terrorists, linked to more than 400 deaths, and subject to Scotland Yard warrants, an Interpol Red Notice, and known as 'The White Widow', placing her in the league of the Chechen female suicide bombers, the 'black widows'.

In 2012, Kenyan police, after talks with Scotland Yard, issued an arrest warrant for Lewthwaite, who was using the name Natalie Faye Webb and travelling on a fake South African passport. She remains wanted for terror plots with Al-Shabaab, a terrorist group from the UK operating across Somalia and Kenya. She was involved in an attack on a bar in Mombasa, crowded as fans watched Euro 2012, and linked to an atrocity which killed 71 people in Nairobi. It was reported in 2025 she is being protected by terrorist groups in Somalia. I still can't comprehend how, when she was pregnant, she sent her husband off to kill himself and a whole bunch of innocent people. How can you be indoctrinated to do that?

Similarly, the other teenage 7/7 bomber, Hasib Mir

Hussain, a quiet lad apparently who was still living with his parents in Holbeck on the outskirts of Leeds when he became a mass murderer. Like Khan and Shehzad Tanweer, he was a second-generation British citizen, and his family were of Pakistani origin. He went to the Matthew Murray Secondary School in Leeds and was involved in racially motivated fights. He left school in July 2003 with seven GCSEs and went on to study an advanced business course, which he finished a month before the killings.

A year before leaving school, Hussain went to Mecca to do the Hajj pilgrimage and went to Pakistan to visit relatives. On his return to the UK people saw he was more religiously observant, and he grew a beard and began to wear robes. He wrote 'al Qaeda – No Limits' on his religious education schoolbook. He would speak openly of his support for al Qaeda and said he believed the 11 September bombers were *martyrs*.

His life became attending local mosques and youth clubs in Beeston where he fell in with Khan and the others. As they plotted, Hasib Hussain suddenly stopped dressing in traditional robes and took on everyday Western wear. In July 2005 he told his family he was going on a trip to London to visit friends and when he failed to return, his parents reported him as missing to police. He'd boarded the No 30 bus in London armed with enough explosives to rip the double-decker apart, killing 13 people. His driving licence and cash cards were found in the wreckage. I wonder always what they all thought they were doing and when Khan appears in my dreams and darker moments it's a shame he won't answer.

Still, I doubt any of them would have adequate explanations. I struggle with that all the time, for there are always questions. Some people are so weak and are looking for something, be it just absolute notoriety. Unfortunately, the recruiters for al Qaeda and ISIS and all the terror groups are good at picking on the weak – they're not the ones putting bombs on their bodies.

I have always been astounded by the very fact that somebody sat down with Khan and said: 'We think it's a good idea that you get all these chemicals together, put them in a pack, put them in a bag, get on a train and blow yourself to Kingdom Fuck.'

And he went: 'Alright, then. Crack on.'

I'd be saying, you go first and let me know how it goes but Khan went blindly on. I don't get it when he's got a wife and children, and he knows that he's walking out that front door leaving them. The power of brainwashing is astonishing.

Khan was a teaching assistant, a pillar of the local community, everyone knew him, and he couldn't do enough to help people. He got talking to a bloke in a mosque one day and the guy told him about the British and American soldiers raping and torturing women and invited him to a meeting in the basement of an Islamic bookshop where he was given 'inspiring' material and played videos; over time they got into his head and he left his mosque, went to the recruiter's mosque and began spouting radical views.

This mosque kicked him out and he went to another, and he got kicked out of that one and then a third mosque welcomed him with open arms. I think the issue we have, and why it's never going to be resolved, is because the starting point to resolve it has to come from within the community. Those mosque leaders who were alarmed that Khan was a huge Mr Nutty Bar and banned him from attending should have called the police: 'We've got this guy and we're frightened that he's going to do something so surveillance might be a good idea.'

There are audio recordings of Khan talking to a man about the 7/7 attacks and he says: 'I can't do anything until the end of June because my wife is expecting our baby daughter, and I need to be able to say goodbye to her.'

He was already prepared for the attacks months and months in advance and he knew it was a one-way trip he was taking. There's a video of him holding his son and telling him he is going to be a martyr and a hero of Islam, and Allah will shine down on you and your mother, and I will always be there and wait [for you].

When he detonated the bomb, there was no fear, there was no hesitation, he looked at me, looked down the carriage, looked at me again, stared at me as he sat back and put his hand in the bag. There was no screaming or shouting, no fuck all. He was calm. I think one of the most terrifying things is that he was that okay with it; that he looked along the train and saw all those people and thought: *I'm going to kill you. I'm going to kill all of you.*

It still makes me shiver. And Hasib Mir Hussain who blew up the bus? The plan that day was to hit four trains and for Hussain to blow up on the Northern line, but that line was shut because of a signal failure. After the bombers split up, and the other three were on their trains, and he couldn't get on his train, Hussain walked outside the station, and telephoned Khan the ringleader.

But Khan was already in bits. There are 52 missed calls in ten minutes from Hussain's mobile to Khan's number trying to find out what to do. What would any right-minded suicide bomber do? He walked down Euston Road to Burger King and had breakfast. He sat there and he ordered his breakfast and ate it and put his bag down on the floor. If somebody had kicked it half the street would have gone up in flames. There's CCTV footage of him leaving Burger King and walking along the street. He stops at King's Cross Station and looks inside the bag; he crosses the road, and he goes into Boots and buys a new 9-volt battery because the battery on his device has died. He changes the battery, walks out to the road and the first thing that comes along is a bus. He gets on it.

It's all supernatural, the calm. There's CCTV footage from a service station where the bombers stopped on their way from Leeds. In the trunk are about 20 homemade explosive devices, like mini-grenades, and a gun. Their plan was to shoot if they were stopped by the police, cause chaos whatever happened. With this bomb-laden car, guess what? They stop at services for fuel and buy drinks and sandwiches. Who the hell is hungry when you're going to blow yourself up? How could you be fucking hungry, knowing what you're going to do?

Khan pays for the fuel and drinks and sandwiches. The woman cashier gives him his change. He stands there and counts it and says she's shortchanged him by 20p. He demands it, she gives it to him, and he leaves. It wouldn't surprise me if he'd asked for Nectar points. It beggars belief that he'd stand there and argue over pennies.

The last CCTV of the four together is at King's Cross Station where they all hug each other and say a little prayer and then off they go, oblivion awaits but you'd never know it. The normality of how you see them is the most disquieting. Hussain couldn't get on his assigned train, the other devices have gone off, and he could have put his bag back down and walked off and the others would never know. But he sat on the back of that bus and he looked around and ten minutes into the journey he blew up. I can't ever reconcile that.

People talk about forgiveness, and I think that's fucking insane. If you forgive that you're as bad as them as far as I'm concerned. The total frustration is never being able to understand the reasoning. I was tortured by this for years. I'd replay the moment Khan set off the bomb and wonder if it was something I did that made him act at that moment; the way I was dressed, a look in my eye? Was it me? Was I the trigger?

The only way I moved on with my life, and it took a

long time, was to compartmentalise it, understand mad people do bad things. That's it. That's all you can say. It's no different to the old *Blackadder* TV series when he puts his underpants on his head and pencils up his nose pretending to be mad because he doesn't want to go over the top. It's a level of insanity that they take to the nth degree. It's a madness and a very real one.

Today I do understand mind games from an education that began in the tunnel. I was wide awake. As I was when they wheeled me into hospital screaming and shouting. It's a dreadful Catch-22. If I'd passed out, I wouldn't have the memories which haunt me. But would I be alive?

The brainbox is amazing: it was staying alert to keep me fighting to live and now it attacks with nightmares. It's my absolute saviour and hero on one hand and it's my absolute nemesis on the other. Why fight so hard to keep me alive and then haunt me, where's the fairness in that? In the immediate years after 7/7, surviving didn't seem like a blessing, it felt like a punishment, every day a punishment. Now, every day is tough going but I count my blessings. It's a different life than I ever imagined I would have but I've discovered it doesn't have to be worse. It made me think outside the box, to find solutions to problems I'd never encountered before. And situations, like meeting the then future King and confronting my Complex Post Traumatic Stress on the same day.

Chapter Six

ROYAL INVITATION

*'You don't have to control your thoughts, you have to stop
letting them control you.'*
– DAN MILLMAN, 2023

WHAT'S IT LIKE TO nearly die? What's it called? A near-death experience? What's that like?

It's a question the well-meaning stumble around but not one which troubles me. I have no great vision of what's on the other side even if I've had more than a glimpse. From my experience during the times that I 'died', I certainly think there's something but not a guy with a long white beard. That said, I'm not a religious person – more of a religious hypocrite.

In the tunnel I was praying to every deity going. The only assurance I can offer is that life and death is not determined by how indomitable the spirit is, but by the beating of your heart. And, I like to think, good intentions to all.

Of course, and you'll fully understand why, I question

what kind of God we're meant to believe in. What kind of God would allow these four animals to get on these trains and that bus instead of blowing up on the motorway when there's no one around them? What kind of God lets monster killers survive to old age in jail while children die of cancer? Where does the logic in that come from?

I'm angry at the injustice of it all.

I'm angry at the ideology behind what put me in my situation. I think that's the thing. I think the anger comes from the sense of injustice, the sense of stupidity behind what Khan did. For, and this will sound strange, I'm a firm believer that terrorism has a 100 percent failure rate. Yes, people get killed and people get injured like me but that isn't the aim of terrorists. Their mission is to terrify people, so they stop living the way they want to.

Yet, the next day after the London bombings people got up and went to work and did all the things they normally would. Khan didn't change anything except kill random people and ruin innocent lives. Tony Blair as Prime Minister didn't say: 'Oh, fuck it, let's bring the soldiers out of the Middle East.' Khan changed nothing.

For me, in the space of 30 seconds I came face to face with the worst of humanity with the animal that did it, and face to face with the best of humanity with Adrian, who saved me. Khan didn't change Adrian's mentality of wanting to help people, he didn't destroy that in Adrian, because Adrian went back in the tunnel and saved another ten people. Terror doesn't work. When are these people going to realise that what they want to create, a fear and terror which affects the economy and stops this country and other countries operating as they want, doesn't happen?

One of the first doctors to treat me was a Dr Ahmed, and he was phenomenal. He is what you'd call a proper Muslim-looking guy with the long beard, the works. What's sad, when I look back on it, is when he finished work that day, put his stuff in his rucksack and went off to catch the bus and Tube, people wouldn't sit near him. They saw his brown skin, his beard and rucksack and feared him. Yet, if any outrage happens, that's the bloke you want because he was unbelievable as a doctor. So, what did Khan achieve? He didn't stop London from being the centre of the country and the economic force that it is or stop people eating out and socialising and clubbing. Did he make the life of Muslim people like Dr Ahmed a million times harder? Absolutely.

Call that a victory. Yes, people died, but many more went to work the next day. It was steely determination. Many people said: 'Let's go for a night out in London and show these fuckers.' Which was the exact attitude after the London Bridge stabbing attacks on 29 November 2019 when two great lives were lost, and three others were cruelly injured. The next night the restaurants and pubs around London Bridge were like party central. There is a bit of nonsense about the *Bulldog Spirit*, people have to go to work, pay their mortgages, but there's a percentage who make the point of going out in protest – *you won't change the way we live.*

You can kill people, maim them, terrify them, but remember what happened after the bombing on 22 May 2017 following American pop singer Ariana Grande's concert at the Manchester Arena? Salman Abedi and his brother Hashem killed 22 people and injured 1,017. It was the worst act of terrorism and the first suicide bombing in the United Kingdom since I got blown to bits. What happened? Crowds packed the next concert; audiences went back because they are living their lives. You live with that threat, particularly in London.

Years ago, it was the IRA – I heard the Canary Wharf [1996] bombing, it was near to our house – so Khan and the boys were simply new guys on the block, new guys with the bombs. It's the way it's done that's new. On the Tube or the bus, you can't tell the good from the bad. I didn't look at Khan and think 'fuck me, he looks a bit suspicious' for, on the face of it, he was a young Asian guy with a rucksack. And no more than that. People go on to me about peace treaties but if you got shit bag bombers like them around a negotiating table they'd just blow it up.

I blame Khan for what happened to me on that day and for the years he's been clambering in my window or crawling up my bed, for the minutes and hours and days he has contaminated my mind with his poison. I don't blame the Muslim community. Being a big East End lad, after the bombings some UK right-wing extremists thought I'd be up for it and tried to recruit me as a spokesman and anti-Muslim figurehead. I told them I was the victim of a murderer, someone as close to a true Muslim as a Ku Klux Klansman is to Christianity, and not to let the door hit them on the way out. I didn't want extremists to feed off my story, make me their poster boy. I was asked to talk with leaders and speak at several events but there was no way I was going to do that.

One of the reasons I'm still alive is because of doctors and nurses who are practicing Muslims. If you look over the past 20 years every terrorist attack has been Islamic related so some people simply say all Muslims are terrorists. What about the IRA? Are all Irish people terrorists? If I had done any of that it would only have stirred up trouble and then you create a never-ending cycle. But I'd be lying if I said I was all benevolence, for if I ever had the chance to beat the shit out of Khan, I would indeed believe that was being in heaven.

That I regard as a normal reaction, not the suffering of my turbulent mind which has been with me since the nights in the Zachary Cope hospital ward when Sister Naj held my hand and comforted me during the 3am horrendous night terrors.

There's no escape from PTSD, it's the body's fight or flight response to danger, and it spirals the mind, most certainly mine. On the day when they were rescuing me there was the sound of sirens everywhere and police officers shouting for people to get back, get out the way, stay behind cordons, and firefighters running in and out. The noise in my head was as loud as the bomb going off. If a police car or an ambulance hits the siren when I'm about, it's hell for me. I've been rushed to hospital a couple of times and being in the back of an ambulance is a massive trigger to me. I have high blood pressure so in the back of an ambulance it goes through the roof and I'm on the verge of a heart attack.

You can't be cured of PTSD. There's no miracle drug – they can give you medicine to control anxiety and depression but no cure for the root cause. I'm friendly with a former serviceman, Luke Woodley, who has PTSD and gives talks about it. He told me the best description of PTSD was to think of the structure of the brain having a place for everything: a folder with slots for the gas bill, electric bill, TV licence, and every month the bills come in and have their own unique slot in this little folder. It's perfectly well organised. Then, some bright spark puts all the bills on one bill and this big bill doesn't fit in any of the slots. It's got nowhere to go and flits around slot to slot to slot. That's what traumatic memory does in the brain. The brain doesn't have somewhere to store that memory, so it pushes it from point to point. You can never remove the memory. You can't unplug it like a USB stick and remove the data that's disrupting your brain, which can't cope with that traumatic memory.

The brain gets on fine with happiness, excitement, and as much sadness as you like, but trauma is different because it doesn't fit into one of those slots in the folder. With my PTSD I get depression and anxiety and sufferer constantly from obsessive-compulsive disorder [OCD]. I live in a constant state of heightened alert on everything. And I tell you most honestly, it drives you crazy, crazy. If I leave the house and then wonder if I might have left the power on to the kettle, I *have* to go home and check. Not that I've left the kettle boiling but the plug turned on at the wall. Not a big deal at all but my brain says, hang on, that could fuse, and a spark could hit the tea towel which could burn and that will burn the house down.

Once I'd got to a meeting in central London and as I pulled up outside, I thought, *shit, I think I've left the microwave plugged in.* I had to drive all the way back home to check. I had unplugged it. But my brain wouldn't let me focus on anything else until I *saw* it was unplugged. Not told. Over the years it's become easier and if someone sends me a picture on the phone of the kettle or whatever unplugged I can accept that. Just.

It's all part of the brain seeing normal day-to-day activities, simply going out of the house, as dangerous. In its efforts to protect you it can lock onto some absurd reactions. I never feel safe anytime other than in the confines of my house. Outside, I'm constantly scanning my environment. Is there a bag lying around? If I go to a hotel now, I'm checking wardrobes, I'm moving pillows, I'm looking under the bed, seeing me you'd think I'd been trained by MI6, looking for anything that could potentially hurt me.

If I feel there's risk, I want to neutralise it or get away from it as quickly as I can. I live in a constant state of heightened alert to a threat and that is often one of the most innocuous things possible. If it snows and I'm inside that's all fine, but if I'm outside I fear I might get trapped in a snowstorm, or if it rains get trapped by a flood. It's the thought of being trapped that sets me off because of being stuck down the tunnel. I hate lifts because of that, for if I got stuck in one, I'd smash the Granny out of it to get out. There is no logic involved.

One evening I watched something on Paramount+ about soldiers out in Iraq and there were many IED explosions. I've watched films with explosions and had absolutely no problem. I watched a show fronted by Robbie Coltrane, *Critical Evidence*, about a guy who tried to off his wife with a car bomb. I went to bed, and it was fine. And then, the nightmare that Khan was coming through the window.

I woke up and sat bolt upright in bed, looked around the room and Khan was standing next to the bed. I shut my eyes, thinking it's just a dream. I opened them again and he was still there. I'm in a panic wondering if the house is locked.

I know he's dead. But in my head, for that split second, he's back and wants to kill me. Every time I shut my eyes he is there, and I'm taken back. Was it the Iraq show on TV or the car bomb killer stuff? I don't think so. It goes deeper than that. This was around an anniversary of the murder of the Parliamentary protection policeman Keith Palmer, who was killed when, unarmed, he stopped a knife-waving terrorist getting into Westminster on 22 March 2017. He was posthumously awarded the George Medal (the second-highest award for gallantry).

As part of my work on disability rights and the care of PTSD I give talks and had done that at the Ministry of Justice in London, not long before my nighttime visit from Khan. I gave my talk close to the anniversary of Keith Palmer being stabbed and I had problems with the security allowing me into the venue. There was a lot of stress, and I think that kind of overtly kicks it off, a combination of little things that build and build. And you're back there.

It's really strange, because you can wake up one morning feeling on top of the world and then during the night it all comes crashing down around you and it's a struggle to get out of bed. Because no matter what you do, you're reliving it. You're hearing it, you're smelling and you're tasting it. Seeing these things again, believe it or not, it's not the visual thing that's traumatic. Obviously, it's not pleasant to see but it's the sounds, it's the smells, that does the damage. If you watch a horror film on mute, that's okay, but you watch the same film with the sound on, that stimulates the senses and the combination can bring on the dread and horrors for me. I can suppress the actuality, no matter how loathsome it is, but not the mental horror.

Generally, people don't understand that. It's become a fashion to be 'stressed' by work or by life and that makes it more difficult for those of us truly plagued by it to be taken seriously. Of course, there are many unlucky victims of stress and depression but when it's the real thing it's not cured by a couple of duvet days off work. It dumbs down the agenda.

What I fake much of the time is being okay. When my depression is bad, I go into myself, and I can't do anything. I lose interest in everything, shaving is like trying to park a juggernaut. There's no magic pill and the worst thing is people telling me to deal with it, pull myself out of it. I can't do that: nobody would choose to live the way that I live when my PTSD is bad. I can't control it, it just happens and I have to ride it out. That's why a lot of people drink and turn to drugs looking for any escape to take their headspace somewhere else. With PTSD, I concentrate on work or read or go on my game console and that takes me away for a couple of hours but when I stop or close the book or turn the telly off, it's back. PTSD takes its place in the queue – *I ain't going anywhere, I'm still here*. I'm never more than ten seconds away from the next episode. It could be anything, somebody dropping something and glass is smashed – *that's the windows going out of the carriage*. At the dinner table someone drops cutlery – *that's bits of the train hitting the floor of the tunnel*. There isn't anything that doesn't have a connotation, where my brain twists it back into what happened. I had an explosion, fire, smoke, smells, injuries, a tricky combination of different triggers my brain can go to and fire, each horror just as terrifying as the one before.

It's like going to get a rescue dog from the pound: you get this big Rottweiler and take it out for a walk and this dog's brilliant. It sits when you wait to cross the road, he's right by your side and doesn't bark or misbehave. The next day that same dog shits and pisses everywhere and is trying to drag you into the traffic and biting passers-by. You have no control of that dog whatever. Welcome to having PTSD.

One day I can be okay and in the blink of an eye, I've got no control over what goes on around me and I can't function. It's like trying to control a wild animal that behaves if it wants to. If it doesn't, all I can do is hold on tight and go along for the ride. I'm always tired because I'm constantly battling in my own head to do the most basic of things like go outside my own front door. If I go into a restaurant and there's a birthday party and a kid with a balloon it's a fucking nightmare. I know at any given time, that thing is going to burst and I'm not going to be in that restaurant anymore, I'm going to be on the floor of the tunnel. I can't turn to the kid's parents, saying: 'Sorry, I'm a terrorism survivor, if you wouldn't mind getting rid of that balloon?' It's only a kid with a balloon but my brain is constantly waiting for that explosion.

I get very tense, and I get very worked up, my phantom pain increases, and my physical pain increases because my brain is waiting for that full blast, that impact to hit me. It's like that no matter where I go. I don't want to be treated differently, I don't want anything special, I want people to understand that if I need help, I'll ask for it. And if I ask for it, I'm not doing it to be lazy or to be awkward, I genuinely need help. Yet, so often, disabled people like me are regarded as a nuisance.

Certainly, that was my feeling from some that day in St Paul's Cathedral, on 1 November 2005, when the then Archbishop of Canterbury, Rowan Williams, spoke of the *sense of arbitrariness* created by terrorists targeting people because of where they were at a particular time, and terrorists believed any victim 'was as good as any other'. But he argued: 'There are no generalities for us, no anonymous and interchangeable people. We live by loving what's special, unique in each person. Everyone matters.'

Everyone doesn't listen. One of the things that has always been an irritation to me – I know this might sound horrible, but it's not intended to be – and makes me very frustrated, is when people are terribly injured and then they want to climb a mountain, or jump out of a plane, which is an avoidance of confronting what's happened to you.

I find it more remarkable when people go through something like that, and then try to put their life back together and try to live a normal life.

Yes, jumping out of an aeroplane strapped to somebody takes some balls to do, I'm not denying that. But that's not going into a supermarket where every fucker is looking at you like you're a freak. It's not going out for a meal, and effing people having to move chairs out the way so you can get to a table and making a big kerfuffle about it where everyone's now turning around and looking at you.

Living day-to-day life is harder than climbing any

mountain or jumping out of any aeroplane. My aim after I got hurt was to try to go back to work, to get my life back to some semblance of normality that I had before the bomb and it's been an incredibly tough journey. The pantomime stuff is ten seconds of inspiration for the public and sets a wholly unrealistic precedent for any true understanding of living with disability. I had offers to go on television, one to do *Strictly Come Dancing*, but it wasn't for me. They told me: 'You must want to do it?'

'Why? I couldn't dance when I had legs.'

'But you'd be on television…'

He sounded like that pillock who now does *University Challenge*, and I told him: 'It's not me. I've as much rhythm as a zebra.'

'But you'd be partnered with a professional dancer.'

I explained I wasn't being funny, but I had no intention of chucking whomever her name might be around a dance floor. I asked point-blank: 'Would I look good in a leotard and sequins?'

It was not my thing going out there saying I'd been blown up but now I'm a ballroom dancer. Now, having been a project manager, Kevin McCloud and *Grand Designs* and people creating and building their homes would have suited – and no sequins necessary. Something practical where I could also talk about PTSD and raise awareness around that.

I've had offers to do parachute jumps and all kinds, including climbing Mount Kilimanjaro. Why should I change everything about me because of what's happened and do things I had no fucking interest in doing before I was hurt? What, so I'm disabled, so I'm going to climb a mountain? Trust me, I climb a mountain every day just to get out of bed.

It's the 'mountains' the disabled climb that people don't see that should inspire them, not the literal ones. And so much of that involves a mental struggle. It's present every time the clock ticks and is also an ongoing blight for those who lost loved ones to disaster or terror or found their husbands, wives, sons and daughters returned as damaged goods.

That day in St Paul's, angry as I was at the politicians and their attitude – and like everyone else in the cathedral so aware that the bomb mastermind Khan had cited Tony Blair as the joint architect for the invasion of Iraq as the reason for the suicide attack – I was so aware of the human tragedy. From my corner in the cathedral, the 'nuisance corner' as I thought of it, I witnessed so much of it. Four candles were lit as acts of remembrance representing each of the scenes of the London attacks, the Tube trains at Edgware Road, Aldgate and King's Cross, and the bus at Tavistock Square.

The Queen talked on the steps of St Paul's with some of the families of those killed and she was given a posy by seven-year-old Ruby Gray, whose father Richard was killed in the Aldgate explosion. Her 11-year-old brother Adam refused to attend the ceremony because he blamed Tony

Blair over the Iraq war and for making London a terror target.

Their mother Louise, from Ipswich, told London's *Evening Standard*: 'He is very angry with the bombers, but he also blames the war and he blames the Government. He doesn't want to be part of anything that has Tony Blair there.' What moved me greatly was the presence of Graham and Janet Foulkes, who might have travelled to St Paul's Cathedral by taxi but when they arrived in London from Manchester on 7/7 something made them get on the Tube. Their son David, aged 22, was on my train with them. He'd just joined *The Guardian*, starting a career in newspaper advertising, and it was his first journey on the Tube. And his last. He died in the darkness of the tunnel Adrian and the others brought me out of. He was scheduled to move in with his girlfriend, Stephanie Reid. She was with him and his parents on their Tube journey through London to St Paul's.

'It was spontaneous,' Janet Foulkes told the *Daily Telegraph*, adding: 'I felt it was the right thing to do.' Graham Foulkes said the Tube journey had been disconcerting: 'We saw a bag on its own by the door and we all looked at each other. Then, a man picked it up and there was such a sense of relief.'

Graham Foulkes, like I do now, believes the way to overcome the horror of such adversity is to carry on. It was a tremendous struggle for me when I met him many weeks later. Lots of spirited victims fought for life that day, that 7/7, but their hearts stopped when their son died.

Mine beats on. How or why remains a mystery to me despite more than 20 years to puzzle it out. Yet, each day has been a lesson in living. I got an early class in the good manners, the humility and dignity of that, at Highgrove in Gloucestershire.

In May 2006 I was invited to tea at their home by the then Prince Charles and Lady Camilla Parker-Bowles who were holding an event for the bereaved and survivors of terrorist atrocities. I was a mess and still struggling at Roehampton with Khan climbing in the window and pacing around my hospital bed at 3am. I had not met another survivor or a relative of any victim of corrupted ideology.

The families of the dead? How could I face them? Why had I survived? I was to blame for that – they'd hate me, despise me. Their loved ones were dead and gone and here was me – living proof of what they'd lost. It wasn't only survivors and families of 7/7 that were invited. Others included those from the terrorist bombing attacks on 23 July 2005 in the Egyptian holiday resort of Sharm El Sheikh. The Islamist group Abdullah Azzam Brigades murdered 88 people including 11 from the UK, some of them guests at a hotel wedding.

I didn't bill it as a fun Monday out in the countryside and went along reluctantly but, as it developed, it was an exercise in humanity. We were supposed to meet Prince Charles and Camilla, but her father, Major Bruce Shand, died on Saturday 11 June 2006, and she couldn't be there. The King, then Prince Charles, very much was there. It was strange getting through security and being in the grounds which you don't normally get to see.

In the moment it felt special getting a private tour of the gardens. Suddenly, Prince Charles appeared. I'd always regarded the Royals as kind of very aloof and not really engaging, only playing a part. He was totally the contrary. What astounded me was his memory for information. He knew exactly who every one of us was and what had gone on and it wasn't some aide whispering in his ear in the moment before he said hello. I had a nice chat with him. Ask me what we talked about, and I couldn't tell you. I can only say I did feel better having spoken with him. I've had my share of platitudes during the past couple of decades but even then, I could hear the genuine concern and care in his voice, spot it in his eyes. I can understand people in their eyes. Charles was tremendous, charming, and had a sincerity about him. I know he's had a lifetime at such events, but you can't simply turn on empathy in your eyes and his were bright, they sparkled with it.

It was a real contrast to his uncle, Lord Snowdon, the photographer Anthony Armstrong-Jones. When I was in Roehampton, I had my picture taken by him and what a twat Princess Margaret's one-time husband was. I'd been in the Douglas Bader for about two months, and I'd been interviewed by the *Sunday Times Magazine* [4 December 2005]. They told me Snowdon wanted me to travel to his studio in London.

I told them: 'Tell him to get fucked, because there's no

way I'm going to London. If he wants to take my picture that bad, he'll come here.'

They told me: 'It's Lord Snowdon.'

I explained I didn't give a monkey's one way or another. He then agreed to come down to the Douglas Bader and I'm sitting in this old lecture theatre in the hospital, and he goes: 'For God's sake, will you smile?'

'I got blown up and died a few times – smile for your photos? You've got ten minutes and then I'm going.'

I was told later that the photographs were in focus. That seemed to surprise the editors as it was unusual with him. I don't do well with people that condescending, or think because they have got a title they're so much better than me and I must do tricks. Prince Charles, as was, couldn't have been more encouraging and reassuring.

Back at Highgrove, I was even beginning to feel relaxed, selfishly relieved I'd not been face-to-face with families of those who, unlike me, could not be there that day, when a lady from the Seventh of July Assistance Centre, which was set up after the bombings, walks over to me to say one of the other guests at Highgrove was keen to meet me. Who? David Foulkes' dad. I still relive the moment:

I freak, but I can't say no, for Graham Foulkes is looking over at me as this nice lady is speaking to me. What do I say, what can I say? The Seventh of July lady takes control of my chair and wheels me over toward Graham Foulkes and my mind is turning somersaults desperate to find some words of greeting. I didn't know, honest to God, what to expect.

But I couldn't say no, refuse to meet someone who has lost somebody in something that I survived. And I thought, well, if they blow their lid at you or whatever, it's five minutes and it's done. Just, just do it, I'm fighting the PTSD, I don't want to be back in the tunnel but I'm sure as hell heading there.

'I'm so sorry for what you lost.'

This man, who has lost his son, tells me this while grabbing my hand and arm and warmly holding them. I was ready for him to shout and scream at me for surviving. Subliminally, I wanted him to do that, this man who had lost his only son and all the dreams and ambition he had for him, for David died and I survived under the ground at Edgware Road. I still hated myself for being alive and I couldn't understand how this man could show me such compassion and kindness. He didn't deliver the hate I thought I deserved. He was genuinely happy that I had survived, there was no animosity, it was as if he gave me permission to get on with my life. It broke me because I couldn't, I couldn't get over the compassion from the man. He'd lost his son months earlier in a horrendous, horrendous way, and he was concerned about what happened to me, and what I was going through. It was one of those rare heartbreaking moments where it re-establishes your faith in humanity.

It's one of the memories that stands out saying there is good in this world, and it's not all evil. In the tunnel I came face to face with the absolute worst of humanity, and almost instantly face to face with the very best, with

Adrian; meeting Graham reinforced that in me. That day at Highgrove, my brain, buggered about as it was, didn't find that easy to accept, but today I recognise how saintly Graham Foulkes was to me, for him *everyone* did matter. It made me pause. It was like a slap in the face. I needed to be more self-aware. That is not easy.

When I dream, I have two legs, two eyes and all the other missing and scarred parts of me are perfect. Subconsciously, before I wake properly, I'm still somewhere in the dream, and an able-bodied man. My mind wonders if all that happened was only a nightmare and I'm still *me*, and the dream is the reality. Then, I open my eyes.

In the tunnel, I was all about contradictions: I furiously wanted to survive but, surrounded by corpses, there was the urge to join them, be at rest, at peace, as it were. There was such terror that, and it sounds mad, I all but envied the dead.

I do understand suicidal impulses as an escape from the dread of being alive. My mind, which had fought to keep me awake and alert in the tunnel, was warped. My life was in peril for so long that the sub-conscious panicked and the mental struggle – I thought I was being exterminated – with fatalism and the conscious effort to stay awake brought bedlam into my head. There is little relief and no resolution. I've learned to graciously accept respite when the dreams end, and the brain kicks in.

It's like my body adjusts to an acceptable level of pain and will stay like that for three or four months and then acts up again for another week of it. It's what I call the cost of doing business, the cost of me surviving is this. I pay a heavy price for it every day and don't take that as meaning that I would rather be dead, because I'll tell you about those days and I'm over them. Dead, I wouldn't know how lucky I am to be alive.

It has taken me a long time, many years, to be able to see that and not feel guilty for surviving. I celebrate my birthdays, Christmas, anniversaries. Yes, there are families that can no longer do that and that takes my breath away when I think on it. I do, and they don't. There was guilt and it was irrational and ludicrous and is no longer.

If I'd died, and one of those 52 had survived, I wouldn't want them to feel guilty for being alive.

I'd want them to grab life with both hands and live it to the fullest.

Initially, there were a few snags for me getting started on that mission. The Government's Social Justice Centre, including the Seventh of July Assistance Centre, which was set up to help the bereaved families and survivors, all those affected by 7/7, apparently did brilliant work.

Sadly, it had closed down by the time I got out of hospital.

And I'd demanded to get out early. Of course, I wanted to stand up and walk out; I wanted to put my football boots and goalkeepers' gloves on and run around the pitch. I couldn't even look in the mirror when I shaved because I didn't like what looked back. But I wanted out of hospital otherwise Khan had killed me in a different way.

PART TWO
DAMAGE
CONTROL

'There is always one more notch and four more aces.'
– BOB DYLAN, BILLY 4,
(PAT GARRETT & BILLY THE KID, 1973)

Chapter Seven

ESCAPE?

'Freedom's just another word for nothing else to lose.'
–ME AND BOBBY MCGEE, KRIS KRISTOFFERSON,
JANIS JOPLIN, 1971.

I SWORE I'D BE out of hospital before the first anniversary of 7/7 and I made it, if only just. I wasn't going to be confined for a full year of my life because of that mad bastard Khan. The medical teams wanted me in hospital longer, but I told them I didn't give a shit what condition I was in because I was escaping before that deadline, out before 7/7/2006.

Life in hospital, the confinement, was claustrophobic but, sometimes it did seem like I was in a *Carry On Doctor* movie. Laughter may not heal the wounds, but absurdity can dilute the pain. In the last weeks in hospital I'm on the Zachary Cope, which is on the ninth floor of St Mary's and it's designated a vascular surgery ward. There are people who have lost fingers or toes through diabetes, and there's me plucked up at the end with no legs sitting up in bed watching the telly.

I'd done a story about my survival with the *Daily Mirror*, and it came out on a Saturday, the day after they'd brought in a new patient on the ward. Today his wife is visiting him. She's sitting on his bed reading the paper and I see her look at me, look at her husband, back at me, and back to the paper, which has a photograph of me plastered all over a couple of pages. She starts on him, and I think 'here we go' and I hear her stage whispering: 'Go and speak to him. *Go on.*'

He comes over bold as brass. Mawkishly: 'You the fella in the newspaper?'

'That's me, mate.'

'What's it like to get blown up?'

'Take a seat, and I'll tell you.'

I don't hold back. I get to where I put my hand up to my forehead and put it inside my skull and he's going green-white. He looks as if he's going to be sick and he's speaking through a weak smile: 'That's enough, mate.' And he scarpers.

'There's more if you want,' I say to his vanishing back.

Some of the visitors I had felt awkward and that awkwardness came in many forms, some telling me about the minor injuries they had sustained in every day life, moaning about how much pain they were in, as I sit there thinking: *are you fucking kidding me* and nearly saying, 'Oh I'll move and you jump on the bed you clearly need it much more than me', but for once I hold my tongue.

It's laugh or cry, and I've learned to ride along with most

of it. People don't realise what they're saying and can't always police their thoughts. It was like that in the Douglas Bader unit, where they told the story, probably apocryphal, of when the RAF fighter, a cantankerous bastard, was giving a talk at some very twee girls' school.

He told the little darlings: 'There were two of the fuckers behind me, three fuckers to my right, another fucker on the left.'

The headmistress was almost as pale as my *Daily Mirror* reader. She interrupts, with an explanation:

'Ladies, the Fokker was a German aircraft.'

Sir Douglas Bader sails on:

'That may be, madam, but these fuckers were Messerschmitt.'

Getting back out into the world for me was nothing like those wartime skies, but it had its hazards. I quickly learned to put on a brave, even cheerful face when inside I was boiling over with fear and upset. I've never been easily offended. People and stupidity make me very angry, yes, but I like a laugh at absurdity. I'm one of these types of people that it's difficult to offend. I don't do the shock! horror! you've called me *handicapped* but I'm officially *disabled*. Or some such bollocks. That's for the full wanker kit crowd, you see them at football matches wearing their team's strip head to toe, certain if a player is injured, they'll be called on the field and, with their pint and gut spilling over, score the winning goal.

If I can't take the piss out of my situation, then who exactly can? People have such a fear of saying the wrong thing that they don't say anything at all, so you end up being ignored. And being ignored is far more isolating than somebody saying the wrong thing. A friend visited me in the hospital when my mobility car was delivered. He looked at me and smiled: 'Well, that must have cost an arm and a leg.'

He twigged what he said and was mortified. I smiled: 'Two legs.'

I wasn't offended. I wasn't broken in bits and upset. He was beside himself. I explained that it was simply a turn of phrase, I didn't want anyone pussyfooting around me, that I knew he would never say anything that would deliberately look to cause me upset or harm.

I told him, as I will anyone, in such a situation: 'Get over yourself and crack on.' Able-bodied people so often get into this shit about perception and feelings when the priority needs to be practicalities. There's a great phrase in the American television series *The West Wing* when the President points out that with so many real problems in the world, he's no time for cosmetic ones.

Near me they changed the names of disabled toilets and disabled parking to accessible toilets and accessible parking. And there was this big hooray. I couldn't keep my mouth shut. I told the local worthies: 'Personally. I don't give a fuck if you call it Mr Blobby's Playpen if every publicly accessed building has the correct access, a toilet that's safe for me to use, every car park has the right number of disabled spaces that are marked out correctly and are policed so they're not abused. That makes a difference to my life. Changing the name is a fluffy thing to make others feel good. Deal with the real issues that affect people's lives, and I'll start clapping and cheering, but changing the name of something, give me strength.'

It was practical support I truly needed by the time my dad wheeled me out of Roehampton, but all the support structure set up after 7/7 had gone. There was no counselling, no checking if I needed this or that, there was nothing in place to support me. I nervously tried to make my own way forward; it was incredibly tough. I had to find out for myself who could, and could not, help.

Even those closest to me found it difficult to understand what had happened to me. My father told *The Guardian* on 29 January 2006: 'I'm ashamed to admit it now, but I never saw him as very resilient or tough. Maybe I'm a natural pessimist, but I misjudged him badly. I see things in his character that have come out from this, that I didn't think were there. But I think we have all been changed so much by it. I can also see more goodness in human nature, because of all the care and kindness that people have shown to us as a family.'

I love them to bits, but I don't think any of my family were truly able to deal with the enormity of what happened to me. Or some friends. I contacted a builder mate and arranged to meet for a drink. We're there, talking – well, I'm talking, and this guy is looking into space. He bursts into tears and tells me he can't stand the sight of legless me sitting in the wheelchair. He leaves money for a drink, and he's off.

I texted another mutual mate and told him what happened. Silence. I phone the geezer, and he doesn't answer. Finally, he texted to me and says he can't deal with it either and please don't call him again. It happened a lot. I'd been treated so well in hospital; it was all so unexpected. The nursing staff in St Mary's were phenomenal, apart from one who was removed from my care. She was a Muslim nurse in a hijab which was okay with me but as she was changing the sheets on my bed she said: 'You the man who was blown up?'

'That's me.'

'Don't go blaming the bombers – it's Tony Blair's fault.'

I freaked, Patrick in the bed opposite who heard this was blustering and red in the face. All the other nurses came over and got her away. I couldn't understand why she'd say it – even if she thought it. Why say it? It was a first impression of what life could be like outside the hospital walls, a microcosm of my new life.

I've had many weird and wonderful things said about me – I've been accused of being one of the terrorists and self-harming. One conspiracy theory was that Adrian and I were terrorists, and my device went off and Adrian's failed. While I was attempting to bleed to death in the tunnel, we made up the story about 'the Asian guy with a bomb'. That was online with a petition for me and Adrian to be arrested for murder and conspiracy.

Some nutter got one going that I was born like this and happened to be at Edgware Road and – this makes me laugh – *jumped on the band-wagon. Jumped!?* Another one was that I'd been involved in a car accident and was attempting to make money from my injuries. The greatest one, and this makes Alastair Campbell's dodgy dossier look plausible, is that I don't exist, I'm a figment of the Government's imagination. The Government puppet masters used technology to create an image of somebody to be the worst injured survivor to push forward the agenda for the war in Iraq, a Weapon of Mass Distraction. This stuff was going on throughout 2006 and into 2007.

There's a kaleidoscope of emotions involved in every aspect, every encounter. Embarrassment, shame, pity, fear and people just not knowing where to look or what to say. I've learned so much in the past couple of decades but tolerance is the most important. Many don't acknowledge the disabled because it's too difficult and they would shove it away, under the carpet if they could, more likely away in the garden shed; as long as it's out of sight, it's out of mind. Which is impossible for us, the disabled, for that disability commands the central position in our lives. Even when I came out of the coma and said that I was fully conscious during everything in the tunnel, my dad didn't believe me. He thought I'd gone doolally, lost my mind as well as my legs. It was only when Graham, a paramedic from the tunnel, visited me and told my dad that I was awake the whole time, knew everything that happened, that he accepted that fact. Khan fucked up my family as much as he did me.

Yet, bless him, my dad looked out for me in navigating

Travel card: Here I am at Edgware Station holding the original ticket from that day

Absolutely pristine: My bank cards had melted and gone but my travel card from the day of the bomb was there and it was in absolutely pristine condition. There's not a fleck of blood on it. There's not a bit of soot on it. Or dust or hair or anything. Pristine, dated 07. Jly. 05.

'Many dead': Newspaper stands following the 7/7 attacks

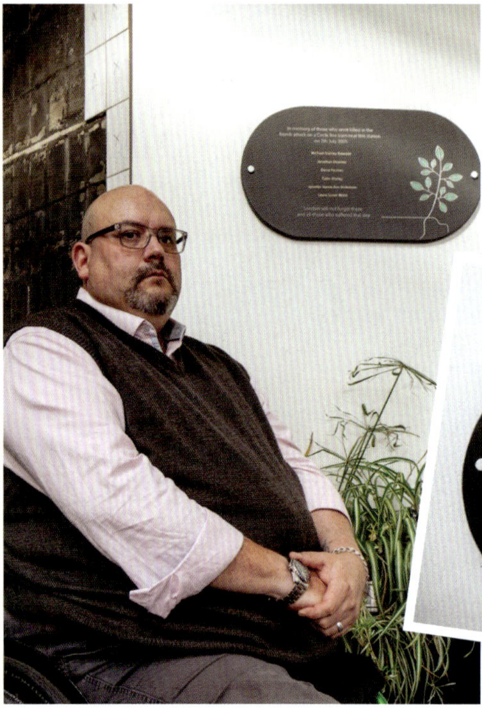

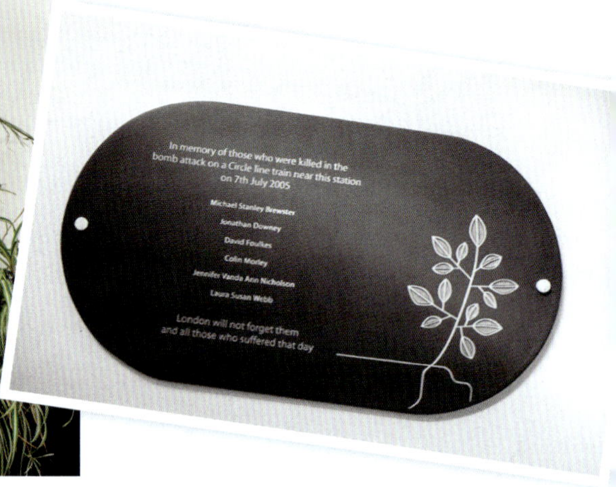
In memory of those who were killed in the
bomb attack on a Circle line train near this station
on 7th July 2005
Michael Stanley Brewster
Jonathan Downey
David Foulkes
Colin Morley
Jennifer Vanda Ann Nicholson
Laura Susan Webb
London will not forget them
and all those who suffered that day

Memorial: A plaque commemorating the victim who lost their lives in the attack. 'London will no forget them and all those who suffered that day'

Bloody good luck: Gem is my saviour. Strange as this may sound, she is the treasure I take away from being blown to bits

District and Circle lines
EDGWARE ROAD STATION
Hammersmith & City lines

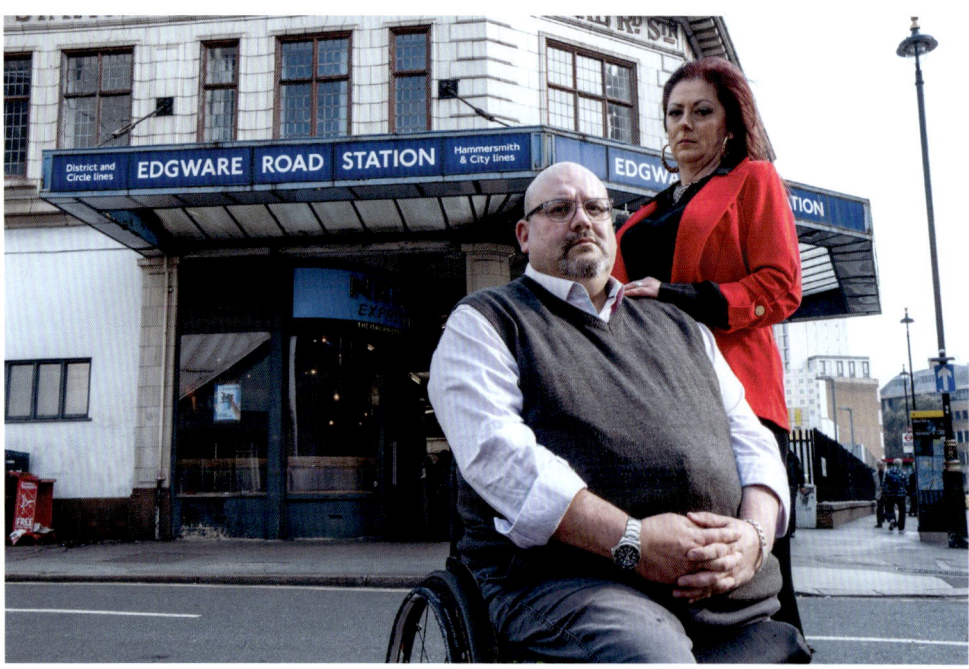

Quoted report: Reading this report, I find it so distressing knowing so little has changed in the Scrooge-like attitude, the meanness, to dealing with the daily threats to lives

Intelligence and Security Committee

Report into the London Terrorist Attacks on 7 July 2005

Chairman:
The Rt. Hon. Paul Murphy, MP

Cm 6785

INTELLIGENCE AND SECURITY COMMITTEE

70 Whitehall
London SW1A 2AS

ISC 105/2006   30 March 2006

Rt. Hon. Tony Blair, MP
Prime Minister
10 Downing Street
London SW1A 2AA

Dear Tony,

On 7 July 2006 fifty-two people were killed in the terrorist attacks in London. The Intelligence and Security Committee has examined the intelligence and security matters relevant to the attacks and I enclose with this letter a Report which covers our findings.

Investigations into the 7 and 21 July events continue, and therefore some information remains *sub judice*. As a result, and on the advice of the Law Officers in consultation with the Crown Prosecution Service, not all of the detail of which we are aware has been included. In laying the Report before Parliament you may wish to consult the Attorney General to assure yourself that the information it does contain will not prejudice current legal proceedings.

The Committee would be grateful if you could lay this Report before Parliament as soon as possible.

Yours ever,

PAUL MURPHY

Blatant errors: Here is the opening letter to the Intelligence and Security Committee Report into the London Terrorist Attacks with the incorrect date

As it happened: Where I was sitting before the bomb went off

The aftermath: Where I landed after the explosion

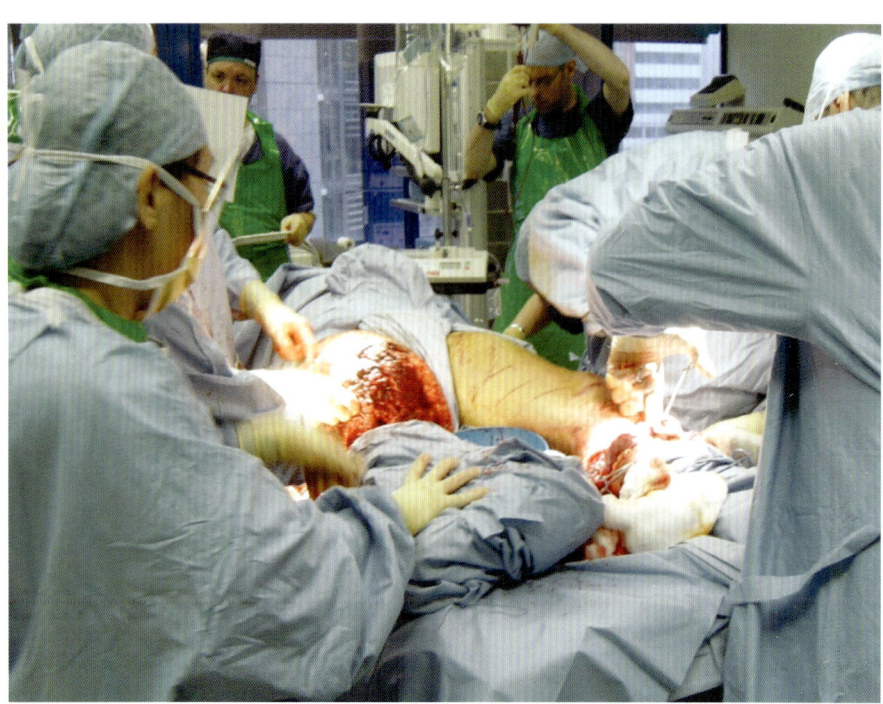

My lifesavers: Four surgeons treated me at the same time. Also present were three theatre sisters, scrub nurses, an anaesthetist, and a cardiothoracic registrar. I was losing blood faster than they could replace it

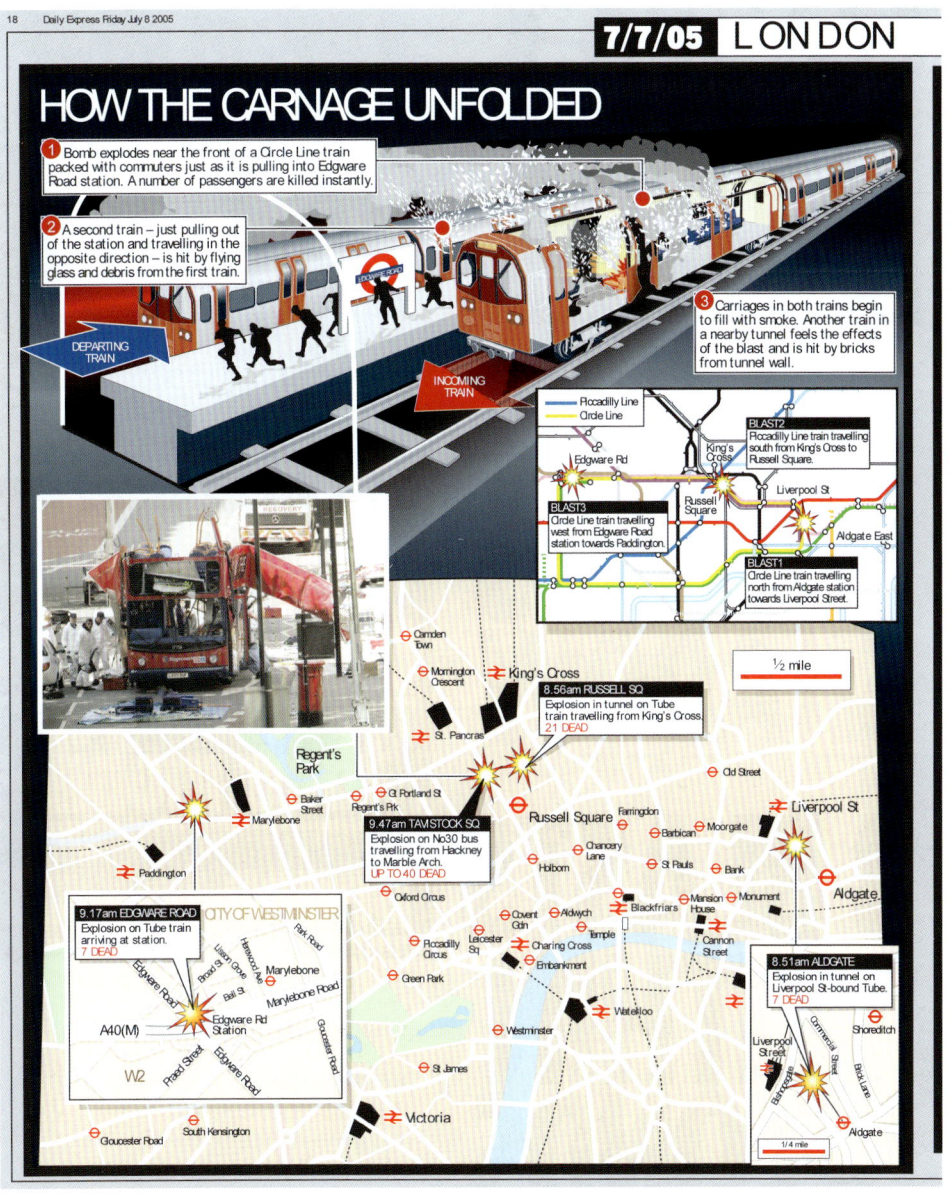

HOW THE CARNAGE UNFOLDED

1 Bomb explodes near the front of a Circle Line train packed with commuters just as it is pulling into Edgware Road station. A number of passengers are killed instantly.

2 A second train – just pulling out of the station and travelling in the opposite direction – is hit by flying glass and debris from the first train.

3 Carriages in both trains begin to fill with smoke. Another train in a nearby tunnel feels the effects of the blast and is hit by bricks from tunnel wall.

DEPARTING TRAIN

INCOMING TRAIN

Piccadilly Line
Circle Line

Edgware Rd

King's Cross

BLAST2
Piccadilly Line train travelling south from King's Cross to Russell Square.

Russell Square

Liverpool St

Aldgate East

BLAST3
Circle Line train travelling west from Edgware Road station towards Paddington.

BLAST1
Circle Line train travelling north from Aldgate station towards Liverpool Street.

½ mile

Camden Town

Mornington Crescent

King's Cross

8.56am RUSSELL SQ
Explosion in tunnel on Tube train travelling from King's Cross.
21 DEAD

St. Pancras

Regent's Park

Baker Street

Gt Portland St

Regent's Pk

Old Street

Marylebone

Russell Square

Farringdon

Liverpool St

Barbican

Moorgate

Paddington

9.47am TAVISTOCK SQ
Explosion on No30 bus travelling from Hackney to Marble Arch.
UP TO 40 DEAD

Chancery Lane

St Pauls

Bank

Holborn

Oxford Circus

9.17am EDGWARE ROAD
Explosion on Tube train arriving at station.
7 DEAD

CITY OF WESTMINSTER

Park Road

Covent Gdn

Aldwych

Blackfriars

Mansion House

Monument

Aldgate

Harrow Rd

Marylebone

Edgware Road

Union Grove

Broad St

Marylebone Road

Ball St

Gloucester Road

Piccadilly Circus

Leicester Sq

Temple

Cannon Street

Charing Cross

Embankment

8.51am ALDGATE
Explosion in tunnel on Liverpool St-bound Tube.
7 DEAD

Green Park

A40(M)

Edgware Rd Station

Praed Street

Edgware Road

W2

Waterloo

Shoreditch

Westminster

Liverpool Street

Commercial Street

Brick Lane

Bayswater Rd

St James

Victoria

Aldgate

¼ mile

Gloucester Road

South Kensington

How it happened: *Daily Express* graphic showing details of the planned attack

WORLD WEEPS FOR US

HOPE IN TERROR'S SHADOW

3 BLASTS WITHIN SECONDS

Tube bombs timed to go off together

'A huge bang, a pile of glass and a mound of flesh landed at my feet '

— WITNESS WALKING ALONGSIDE BUS

We brought the bodies up ...their mobiles began to ring

Breaking news:
Headlines from various
newspapers in the days
following the bombings

Peace: People at a vigil, in Trafalgar Square, London on 14 July 2005 for the victims of the London bombings

In memory: Seventh of July memorial, Hyde Park. A memorial to honour the victims of the 2005 London bombings

Wedding day: 6 June 2015 — the happiest day of my life. Having Gem's support and love makes every day special for me but when we became husband and wife it was such a positive moment to know we'd be facing all the future challenges together

An important but tough mission: On the terrace of the Houses of Parliament with Gem after a day of consultations with Ministers and MPs about accessibility in public places

Dressed to impress: This is the two of us at the black tie National Diversity Awards in 2021 when I was a short-listed nominee

around the bureaucracy which thrives in the aftermath of terror, when the commissions and the inquiries, the paperwork of justification, forgets about the victims. I was 26, the survivor of the worst event to happen in London, probably since the Blitz. And the Government acts as if it's a mugging... *let's not make too much of a big deal of it.* It felt as if we had been pushed to one side, I wasn't looking to be a multi-millionaire – what I lost was priceless – but what I was looking for was some kind of assistance.

My work, TH Kenyon and Co, paid me throughout my time in hospital and kept a job open for me as an estimator. The London British Red Cross contributed money and the lads I played football with generously chipped in. The money helped with getting the right wheelchair and gear for my new existence. I was so grateful for it but what I needed more was encouragement that my life was not now worthless, encouragement of the truth that disability is not an aberration, it's inseparably part of humanity.

Money, of course, is needed for practical needs. Trauma requires more sophisticated currency.

It arrives in all shapes and sizes. And guises, often devalued. National and local bureaucracy will scare the shit out of anybody, and you don't even have to get blown up to qualify. My parents had pretty much lived at the hospital when I was in the coma and when I came out of that, London Transport put them up in a hotel. When I transferred to the Douglas Bader, they found my dad a room in the nurses' quarters so he could be nearby.

He took care of everything; he sorted out somewhere for me to live and a car adapted for someone with my disabilities. The technical problem was more easily solved than the human one. The car was one thing, day-to-day life something altogether different. I was, in real terms, as my house had stairs, made homeless by the bombs in that I needed one-floor accommodation to exist. I'd been renting in Upminster and the local authority was Havering Council in east London. My dad contacted the council housing department and told them my situation, and asked if they could help when I was released from hospital. They told him: 'Your son being blown up isn't really our problem. We are putting people in properties as they become available.

'It might take seven years.

'When he's released from hospital, he'll have to live in a geriatric care home until we find something for him.'

My dad's exasperation got to them. They tried some optimism: 'Maybe not seven, could be five years.'

My dad got in contact with [later Dame] Tessa Jowell, who was a heavy hitter in the Government. She was an absolute darling. She thought getting blown up by terrorist murderers qualified as special circumstances. She contacted Havering Council and told them it was not acceptable:

'You will find this man somewhere to live, and you will do it by the end of the week. Even if you must buy somewhere, you will find this gentleman somewhere to live within two days of this call.'

I was with my dad when they called him. They had a

bungalow – already *fully adapted* to be disability friendly. They'd had it on their books for 18 months waiting for the right candidate. Happy days.

When I went and viewed it, I couldn't get through the front door because there were steps. I had to go through the side gate. There was a ramp at the back to get me into the living room. And once I went through the doorway from the living room to the hallway, which led to the bathroom and the bedroom, I couldn't easily fit through. I squeezed in with my hands down my sides and I scraped and cut all my knuckles, they were really bleeding. All three connecting doorways were too small for me to get through.

The occupational therapist who was there to assess the suitability of the accommodation said: 'We will only widen two doorways.'

I looked at her.

'Hold on. I can go from my living room to my bedroom. What happens if I have the living room/bedroom done, but need to take a piss? I can't get to my bathroom.'

'Well, we are only doing two doorways.'

I indicate that she is being effing stupid.

She insists: 'Only two.'

I'm sitting there with blood still dripping from my scraped knuckles and she says: 'Well, you got through that door.'

I constantly ask myself: *Why are these people making this so much harder?*

There were days when it felt like the people I was dealing with would unplug someone on life support to charge their phone. It seemed my whole journey, from the moment I got out of intensive care, was almost as if everything was designed to be more difficult. There wasn't a simple process. There was no acknowledgment that this was a set of extraordinary circumstances requiring an extraordinary response. I was still in hospital, what I called 'walking school', when I still held hope – something that never, ever vanishes from your mind – of wearing prosthetic legs and getting out for appointments and on weekends. Sense prevailed at Havering Council, and they renovated the doorways, put in a wet room and added a ramp at the front door. By April 2006 I was set up for working from home before it ever became a choice. Of course, I'd have given anything to be going to work – on a building site. That's what I was trained for, construction work.

I was grateful that TH Kenyon and Co, a building contractor based in Bishop's Stortford in east Hertfordshire, kept a job open for me working in contract solutions. I'd only been there three months when I got injured and the day after the bombing, I was due to have a phone call with my boss for my probationary review. It was kind they kept my job open, but I was used to being on site, being outdoors. I felt the four walls squeezing in on me. It was a real kind of culture shock doing the same thing day after day.

I retrained and in December 2007, became a fully accredited consultant for the National Register of Access Consultants and a member of the Chartered Institute of Building. A family friend put me in touch with a company called

Four Group which wanted to create an access and inclusion element of its business and, now qualified for that, I headed that up working with organisations like Marks & Spencer and Transport for London. I was doing quite a lot of work. Again, it was a desk job and the walls came in on me. My dad said stay in the job as getting another won't be easy, but I found position after position searching for something that would satisfy the new me.

I wasn't self-aware enough to know that was because I was a novelty. Every time I went to a new job, I was on more money, and it was great, but it was all because of the notoriety of 7/7 and that diminished, then I wasn't such good PR. Every job I started, my very first day, I'd be photographed sitting outside the office and that would be on their webpage: *most injured 7/7 survivor working for Blah and Blah and Company.*

I heard one of my bosses say that he didn't give a shit if I sat at home watching Jeremy Kyle all day – having my picture on his website was worth 78 grand a year. I was a wheelchair and a set of stubs, and that was good PR for him, and that was it. It was a very bloody time. I told him to shove his shabby job up his arse. Careful was not my modus operandi. Then, I couldn't get a job.

I've distilled a few years there and it had its high moments when I worked on access audits for the disabled for companies like ASDA. But it was a topsy-turvy game, as was my life. I had bad bouts of PTSD and long, long runs of misery. There are bilateral double amputees like me that are done with the world. We've got the same disability, but we've got a different mindset. I'm not criticising the individual that opts out of life, they cope with their disability how they can. But I'm driven to push forward and try and, if I must, fail. It's what I did with the prosthetic legs, I needed the chance. I didn't want to be on my deathbed and not think I'd given it a go. But it was a trial.

My parents lived in the bungalow for a time and others stayed to help. I'd get up of a morning, smile, go to work, feel like shit all day, come home, sit. I used to sit on my driveway, almost preparing myself to go into the house because I couldn't go in there miserable. I couldn't go in there sad, although I lived in this state of almost permanent sadness from not being able to do the things I wanted to do in my head. But the outside world never knew; I remembered what normal looked like, and I could impersonate it really well. I put on the persona of a happy person, not a care in the world. That's not a wise thing to do, to bury the emotions. Internally, it's a fanfare of a horror show when the mask comes off and Khan comes round for an evening. He never speaks, but he's there. And that poor girl crawls up my bed and screams at me for help. Why didn't I help her?

Equally, why didn't the Government, the spooks, MI5, MI6 and all the other branches of the Secret Intelligence Services [SIS] protect us?

I wrote to John Reid [in 2025 Baron Reid of Cardowan] who took over as Home Secretary from Charles Clarke in 2006, but he turned out, for me, to be difficult. I got a very condescending, shitty letter [4 October 2006] in reply from the man. He claimed it was only after the bombings that MI5 'were able to *fully* identify' Khan and Tanweer. A pure play on words. Before him, Charles Clarke, covering his arse before moving on, had maintained the bombers were *cleanskins* – the spooks' term for bad guys previously unknown to authorities.

In the face of extensive HUMINT [human intelligence] from the streets as it were, Reid tried to carry on this farce. My feeling about him was that survivors of 7/7 appeared to be simply a nuisance for him and his office. He held a series of meetings with bereaved families at the Home Office and although I was still in hospital at the time, I was invited to go to one. I rang up to ask: 'I'd love to be able to come but obviously still being in hospital, can you advise me of the best way to get there?'

Speaking to a survivor of a murderous attack on a London Tube train, the woman on the phone tells me: 'There's a Tube stop nearby.'

I made it clear I wasn't happy about that. Later, he refused to meet me. Another time when I contacted John Reid's office to ask whether I could have a short meeting they told me: 'Well, he's a very busy man.' It was the wrong thing to say to me. Before this happened, I was a busy man too.

The day after I got out of hospital, ITV's GMTV show asked me to appear with John Reid to talk about the bombings. I told them he wouldn't appear in person with me – didn't like my questions. And he wouldn't. I did a phone interview, and they wanted to know what questions I would ask Reid. Easy, why wasn't more done to prevent the atrocity when all the evidence was clearly there to know that Khan was a threat?

And how could he justify the operation of the Criminal Injuries Compensation Scheme [CICS]?

Reid, in the TV studio, picked up on the compensation scheme as a lazy escape: 'Obviously, if money is the only issue, nothing can ever compensate for losing your legs.'

What a prick. I wasn't saying money was the only issue but it was one as my whole life has been turned upside down. Right then I didn't know if I'd ever work again. And he turned it around to appear as if I was money-grabbing.

He was a rent-a-quote career politician. More infamy than empathy. There was so much thoughtlessness, and I still wonder why. What were they frightened about, or were they embarrassed and covering up their uselessness? Others didn't even have that excuse. I was arranging a flight and explained my personal circumstances. The lady then went through her tick list:

'Can you walk to the plane?'

I explained again that I had no legs.

'Can you walk to the lavatory on the plane?'

I explained again that I had no legs.

That was all fine, the airline could deal with that. But, just one more question, one more box to tick.

'Can you walk off the plane?'

It was like that on many, many days dealing with

companies and with the Government – I've met every disability minister in the past 20 years and not one thing has come out of it. They all got a nice photograph with me for their websites.

My advice now to anyone dealing with idiocy – don't bottle it up. It's, of course, much worse for survivors of, however provoked, disasters or war. I went through long periods of my life where I kept it all inside and that is agony.

Survivors and bereaved families are going to be incredibly angry. They're going to be incredibly hurt. They're going to feel pain like they've never felt before and it's important that you seek help and you talk to people because I know just how detrimental keeping these feelings bottled up is.

It is a pain like no other. It will never go away – the effect of that day on me will never leave but it becomes manageable, and you develop ways of coping. However, you've got to be able to talk to people and have a really good support network because there are going to be days where you won't want to go on. It can all be overwhelming. As when John Reid's Home Office explained how much my legs, and the other missing bits of me, were worth.

I was told that being so badly damaged the Government got a sliding scale bonus, a play on the supermarket two-for-one deal, in compensating me.

Chapter Eight

THE PRICE IS RIGHT?

'Come on down!'
– BRUCE FORSYTH, BRUCE'S PRICE IS RIGHT,
1995-2000

I'LL NEVER FORGET THE moment. I was at home in the bungalow and sitting at my little desk-office set up when my dad walked in with the post. The first envelope I opened was a cheque and a remittance slip from the Criminal Injuries Compensation Authority [CICA], 2001[1]. I'd died three times in the operating theatre, and I thought the shock might tip me over the edge again. Shock and anger.

It was as if they'd priced my body parts from an Argos catalogue. Without any bedside manner. I was still in hospital when I first got the 54-page Home Office document, a neat A4 ledger of what cash you can get from

---

1   The CICA scheme began in 1964 with the idea victims of crime should be compensated as an expression of public sympathy. Controversy about *compensation culture* in the 1990s forced then Home Secretary Michael Howard to cap total compensation to the extremely rare £500,000.

the Government for *criminal injury*. It's like browsing in the butcher's shop where they've got a diagram of a cow behind the counter all priced up from the prized prime rib to the stewing beef you need strong teeth for. I flipped the pages which are carefully categorised: General, Head and Neck, Upper limbs, Torso, Medically Recognised Illness [Not Mental Illness]. Every bit of you, head to little toe, has a price tag dictated by the Government through the Criminal Injuries Compensation Scheme. I'm the most injured survivor so people think I got millions. I have the begging letters. Not a bit of it.

Head burns – minor visible disfigurement £2,000; Face – moderate disfigurement, £5,500; Neck – severe disfigurement £16,500.

Funnily enough, I didn't qualify for any of that. It was the first mass suicide bombing in the UK, the highest death toll of a terrorist attack in England, but it was treated as if somebody had been knocked off their bike. There was no leeway with the CICA, none whatsoever. I couldn't claim for mental trauma. The response was: 'Well, anybody can say they've got PTSD. It can't be proven.'

Are you fucking kidding me?

And then they deduct money off you for having more than one injury. The nation will only compensate you for three injuries. They're pricing bits of my body that I had been fondly attached to, in every way. My limbs were part of who I was. They also take a discount as I was so smashed about. I got blown up and suffered all these injuries but come on down and take your pick of three to claim for.

It's David vs Goliath. Victims against the System. When I played football, winning was the single outcome.

In life, especially this new life, I've discovered it's whatever you decide winning might be.

A cheque for £118,760 has never felt like a win[2]. Yet, they almost made me feel like I should feel grateful. When I pulled it from the envelope and scanned it with my one eye [I wear a brown prosthetic left eye which perfectly matches the one the doctors saved] it detailed that I got £110,000 for losing both legs. They counted me losing both my legs as one entry. My eye, as a *second* injury, was rated at 85% compensation, £8,100. My absent spleen came in at £660. Nothing for being deaf in one ear or the chemical burns on my arms or the scars – but I don't resent them so much as that's where the surgeons plunged their hands into me and kept me going against all the odds. I had two heart attacks and have permanent lung damage. I died three times in the operating theatre. But they can't financially assess, *prove*, trauma?

Here was the cheque and I'm thinking of the future, of the money already spent adapting a car, buying a wheelchair and all the rest that adds up in the arithmetic of a life

---

2   The Criminal Injuries Compensation Authority treated claimants as victims of crime, basing awards on its existing table of injury payments. Total awards: £2.24 million; average award for death: £17,262; for injury: £6,094; Claimants waived right to sue.

being devastated. I was 27 years old. I was never going to see that sum of money in my lifetime; I sat there looking at it thinking: *Give me my legs back and you can have it back.* I'm holding a cheque for 110 grand plus and part of me wanted to put it in a bin, because I believed it was an insult. I was working in Scotland in 2024 and a lady there was attacked on the street, punched in the face, and suffered a broken nose. She received £2,000 from the CICA. I'm saying it doesn't add up. To help give some sense, if there is any, to the system for you, I'll report what journalist Rob Blackhurst outlined after I talked to him in 2006 about the CICA. He'd studied it for a *Financial Times* analysis of the Criminal Injuries Compensation Scheme:

> *In Glasgow and London, 480 civil servants weigh up, measure and label the suffering of the 65,000 applicants to the Criminal Injuries Compensation Authority each year and distribute £165m of taxpayers' money. They use a price list with hundreds of descriptions of different injuries, ranging in seriousness from £1,000 for a broken finger to £250,000 for quadriplegia. To calculate the amount due, they read down the list and, using submitted medical evidence, decide whether an injury is 'minor', 'significant', 'serious' or 'permanent'. The theory is that if you are a victim of violent crime – whether you were punched by a mugger or injured in the London bombings – you will be treated in the same way. Lawyers describe the system as a 'cheap and*

cheerless' means of compensating for crimes where there is no realistic likelihood of suing the perpetrator. It is not expensive to administer [£305 a claim on average] and relatively simple for victims to understand. But the no-frills approach also means it can be grindingly slow and very rough in its approximation of justice.

Rob pointed out that the Government, knowing the system needed reform, understood quickly after 7/7 that the public perception of a slothful CICA would be poor. The Home Office – our old friend John Reid – oversaw a 'fast-track' and brought in half a dozen specialists. Six! Even then they couldn't change the payment system outlined in my black and white ledger without an Act of Parliament. In 2006 the basic compensation paid for death from violent crime was £11,000; you got the same for total loss of smell or taste, seriously impaired speech or permanent whiplash. If you're a goner, each close relative, as in spouse or child, got £5,500. And it was, and is, complex to pursue other means of financial support.

One of the 7/7 survivors pointed out: 'I've got a colleague who hit a lump in the road and fell off his bike. He got compensation from the council. But how can you sue a man who blew himself up?' Khan hadn't left my life but in payback terms he was gone, gone, gone.

The CICA allows claims for injuries and lost earnings up to the half a million-pound limit; a big-earner business-man would get more than me for the same injuries. While

THE PRICE IS RIGHT?

I was recovering, some survivors, not hurt as severely as I was, and relatives of the dead and injured, marched on 10 Downing Street in protest about the compensation.

On paper it was a cruel contrast to how the victims, in every sense, of the 9/11 terrorist assault in America were looked after: the average award for death was a little more than $2 million and for physical injury it was $393,000. The highest 7/7 compensation was £141,050 and the lowest award was £722 for funeral expenses paid by a friend or relative. I can't confirm for sure, but I'm told the total compensation paid for 9/11 (2,973 dead, 4,400 injured), calculated on a case-by-case basis, was more than $4 billion. For 7/7 (56 dead, 700 injured) the UK paid £2.72 million. By taking the money, you forfeited any further claim for compensation.

The now defunct *News of the World* got all hot and bothered for us with squealing headlines and created *What About the Victims?* placards for protests and got rent-a-quote MPs to ask pointed questions in the House of Commons. And, wow, the paper went for it with: *TRAGIC victims of the 7/7 London bombings are to have their compensation payments DOUBLED, the News of the World can reveal.* Bollocks.

The Sunday paper printed a letter: *It's great to see the Government doing right by the 7/7 survivors.* Politics. The *News of the World* said that compensation was going to be doubled. But after that article we found out that ever so quietly the Government were implying we would get a

50 percent increase in compensation rather than double. Sadly, the added £59,380 this would have meant for me never materialised. It was the same old story – headlines, noise, promises and then sweet fuck all happens. Either financially or any other way. I heard the tired phrase 'lessons will be learned' so many times it's an earworm. I should sue for tinnitus.

Being disabled is not cheap. Twenty years on I receive what used to be called the disability living allowance, now a Personal Independence Payment (PIP). Every disabled person across the board gets some level of PIP. It's not means tested. I don't claim any other benefit. I don't claim housing support, I don't claim income support, I don't claim Employment Support Allowance, I don't claim Universal Credit. I have the one benefit which every disabled person is legally entitled to. I don't claim anything else. So, if I don't earn, I can't pay the rent. I've always paid my way – that's not to say I'd reject help – but I can't sit back and cry 'poor me' and not try to help myself. I'm too proud for that, often to my detriment.

If I claimed Universal Credit, I could theoretically only work 16 hours a week as I believe you can only earn £12,750 a year before it affects the benefit you get paid. I'd rather work for my money, and I make more than that but only just and it's below the threshold of paying tax. The PIP payment allows me to be independent and live independently. It pays for my specially adapted car but it's not a freebie, they take £350 a month off me to pay for the car.

I get £400 a month, to help pay for wheelchairs and any additional things I need. The problem as the years go on is that I must increasingly find more cash for the costs of being independent.

When I left hospital on 30 June 2006, the NHS provided me with a wheelchair. It was made-to-measure, the works. I picked the chair I wanted. The NHS paid for it. Now I get a £50 voucher for the wheelchair I'm sitting in at this moment and it costs £3,500. I need a new one. I can't afford it. A 50 quid voucher is your lot – and the cushion I sit on, it's just a bit of fucking sponge, costs £65.

I use a *sports* wheelchair which has no arms or back, I can't lean back. The advantage is that it's lightweight and enables me to independently transfer in and out of my car and put the chair in the car. I'm in it for sometimes 18 hours a day and I'm slouching all the time. That's not good for all the internal riots going on with me so I investigated getting a bigger chair with a high backrest and armrest. A guy from a mobility company did an assessment and showed me a chair which I liked. I thought it might run to £500 but they wanted £1,500 which I don't have lying around – or the £3,500 to replace the worn chair I'm in now. If I get a puncture, it's £45 a tyre, plus £15 for an inner tube.

I have tape on the wheel rims I use to push. They had a rubber insert running all the way through the middle of it – in the wet you can get some grip – but it broke down, the insert's gone and it's a U-shaped channel. Without the tape

I'd cut my hands to bits. To replace the rims, just the rims, is £800. They give you 50 quid, and then make you feel like they're doing you a favour. The world revolves around a *computer says* agenda.

Charles Clarke, Home Secretary on the day of 7/7, maintained that in terms of compensation all crimes were the same. 'Whether you are stabbed outside the pub or maimed by an explosion on a Tube train, it's not actually the way in which you are injured that is the key thing – provided it's a criminal act – but the extent of the injuries.'

He got knocked by his boss Tony Blair, more the plausible bollocks political animal, who told the Commons that the bombings were 'wholly exceptional' and that us victims required 'additional support'. There was so much hot air, but the CICA system needs to be there. It is designed for someone who gets knocked over in the street, not for someone who gets on a train with a mad bomber like Khan. There needs to be an alternative system for when something like 7/7 happens but as far as I'm aware victims would be in the same sorry old mess if another outrage took place tomorrow. The moment Khan stepped into that carriage, I entered a warzone, and I didn't know – and I had no protection. You elect a Government to protect the people it governs. The Government failed badly. Lessons will be learned. My arse.

What I am still learning, and this is so many years on, is about the desperation of the Government and the security services to distance themselves from 7/7. I repeat what I pointed out earlier: if everyone had been killed on 7/7 I think it could have been dismissed as three electrical faults on the Tube and an engine explosion on the bus. It would simply have been more convenient.

I and the other survivors would have been less of an embarrassment. But I am here to say that Khan and his mates should have been arrested a long time before they killed and maimed so many, many people. A protective shield was put around the activities of the bombers – their training in al-Qaeda camps in Pakistan for seven weeks, the recruitment of sympathisers in the UK – as a way of defending the mishaps of British Intelligence.

They had surveillance photographs of Khan in a training camp in Pakistan in warrior mode with full beard and bandana but when witnesses were asked to identify Khan preparing for 7/7 he had shaved and was in 'civilian' guise. They knew who the bombers were who carried out the attack within two hours of the explosion. The defence MI6 put forward was they knew they posed an imminent threat, but they believed the imminent threat would be on foreign soil not in the UK; that they were planning a terrorist attack in another country. And therefore, didn't warrant the expenditure for surveillance in the UK.

The culpability lies with the security service. They knew who they were. I was told that they were able to identify all four bombers quicker than they could identify me, and I had all my ID on me. The bombers swapped IDs to try to confuse the investigation process, but they still identified them. It took them 19 hours to find out who I was. It was a cruel misjudgement on the part of the spies and their Whitehall masters who didn't do their job properly.

There was never a public inquiry into 7/7, which there was after the 2017 Manchester bombing. Nobody has been held accountable for those failures. It's a joke when you fast forward a dozen years to Manchester and the Ariana Grande concert bombing and more *lessons will be learned*. What was said after the public inquiry was almost verbatim from the aftermath of 7/7. Precautions would be better, and the survivors would be cared for. Tony, one of the survivors of 7/7, with all the horror made real to him again, killed himself in despair after Manchester. There should be an emergency and mental health service that kicks in when we have mass atrocities, but we don't have it. We just expect people to clog their way through.

Tony was on the same train as I was at Edgware Road, but he was a few carriages back; when the bomb went off, he got off the train uninjured, didn't see anything, got onto the platform and made his way out of London. He worked for a law firm in Manchester. After the Ariana Grande concert attack on the Monday, Tony didn't turn up for work the next day, which people said was really unlike him, single guy and diligent in his work. A no-show was unheard of. When he didn't appear on the Wednesday, they telephoned his sister who went to his flat. She opened the door and found him dead. He'd killed himself. The note he left said: 'If we can't learn the lessons of 7/7, I don't want to live in this world anymore.' And it broke my heart, because I knew exactly where he was coming from, how he was feeling, and I was lucky that I had the support system around me to help me through that time. And he didn't, and he wasn't able to reach out to the mental health services for whatever reason, and he killed himself.

I always firmly believed that the death toll of 7/7 should now be 53 and not 52, because he may not have been killed on the day, but every day since, a bit of him was dying as a result. It never ends. We get the platitudes but not the answers.

In July 2021, Eve Aston, an Ariana Grande fan who attended the Manchester Arena concert, was found dead in her bedroom at home in Finchfield, Wolverhampton, after experiencing depression and PTSD in the years after the bombings. She was 20 years old. Her parents said she struggled with loud noises and sleeping following the bombings. I can so understand how she was so severely troubled. As many were by the atrocity at Manchester. An inquiry into the police and security response to the Manchester Arena attack said 'a series of failures' cost lives on the night. The big one for me was that, quoting the inquiry findings, 'notably there had been multiple opportunities to identify the suicide bomber, Salman Abedi, as a security threat'.

I know it's complex protecting the nation, there are many different ramifications and the intelligence service and officers have a really difficult job, but if you make a mistake, you've got to be held accountable for it. Otherwise, how does anything ever change if they've got carte blanche to make mistakes?

People had their lives irreversibly changed in ways that most people can't begin to imagine but there was no sanction for the mistakes which brought that on. In any other walk of life, if you make a mistake and people die, you are held accountable. This isn't *Slow Horses* or some other spook television series where it's all make-up and fake blood and no one gets hurt.

I was still in Roehampton when I began my own inquiries into the bombings and the bombers around April 2006. That's the date of the Intelligence and Security Committee 'Report into the London Terrorist Attacks on 7 July 2005'. The Chairman was the Rt. Hon. Paul Murphy, MP, and he presented the report with an official covering letter to the Prime Minister, Tony Blair. The now ennobled Murphy (Baron Murphy of Torfaen) enraged me and many others. In his letter to Blair, this Lord Slapdash Murphy got the date of the attack wrong – 'on 7 July *2006, 52* people...' it was, in this case, quite literally insult to injury.

He couldn't even check his own letter. It emphasised that none of them really cared. I was sitting on my hospital bed when I read that opening line. I thought: *how can I trust this document when they can't even get the bloody year of the bombings correct?*

The report with that letter went to every injured person and to the bereaved from 7/7. It was a kick in the teeth to me and I can only imagine how this farcical nonsense must have hurt those who lost their loved ones.

It really is tough reading. I sat down with a highlighter pen and a Biro, and I went through it. I didn't really sleep until I got to the end and back a few times. It was that distressing. I then spent weeks going through it, repeatedly.

What annoys me the most is the fantasy that Khan and the gang were *cleanskins* before the bombs exploded all around London. I was told the security services had an audio recording of Khan talking to a guy who was part of the network that helped organise 7/7: Khan is telling him he can't do anything until the end of June, possibly the beginning of July, as his wife is expecting a baby.

That's all on tape before 7/7. It's clear the authorities know that there's an imminent attack, and that it's going to happen when June runs into July. *Cleanskins*?

The inadvertent role Khan's expectant wife played in 7/7 was made clearer to me in later years when it was suggested that the attack on London was aimed at stopping the city winning the 2012 Olympic Games, the very thing I was celebrating the day before my life changed forever. Scotland Yard later found evidence that the attacks were planned for the morning rush hour of 6 July 2005.

Investigators discovered a 6 July text message sent from Khan to the other bombers delaying the attack: 'Having major problem. Can't make time. Will ring you when I get it sorted. Wait at home.'

Khan's wife had had a miscarriage in the night. Panicked,

the bombers wanted to keep their devices cool and bought sacks of supermarket ice, shown on a receipt found after the attacks, and registered at 5.27am on 6 July 2005. There is CCTV of Khan and Shehzad Tanweer buying the ice, with their original plan thwarted.

The International Olympic Committee [IOC] meeting in Singapore, began voting for which city would get the 2012 Games at 11.26am UK time, about three hours after the original time for the attacks. It's a good bet there would have been no London Olympics if the bombs had gone off as planned.

Khan and Shehzad Tanweer knew what they were about. Their trips to and from Pakistan to learn bomb-making dovetail with when London's Olympic bid was first made, and the IOC visits to London during the process. And these two were on the radar.

The spooks knew they were dangerous, knew they posed the threat.

The authorities could have arrested Khan and co long before they became killers.

They could have lifted Khan and stopped 7/7 from ever happening.

Chapter Nine

INTELLIGENCE?

'Until we have a better relationship between private performance and the public truth, as was demonstrated with Watergate, we as the public are absolutely right to remain suspicious, contemptuous even, of the secrecy and the misinformation, which is the digest of our new.'
– *JOHN LE CARRÉ IN INTERVIEW, 1979*

HERE IS THE OPENING letter to the Intelligence and Security Committee Report into the London Terrorist Attacks:

From: The Chairman, The Rt. Hon. Paul Murphy, MP
ISC 105/2006
Rt. Hon. Tony Blair, MP Prime Minister
10 Downing Street London SW1A 2AA, 30 March 2006
INTELLIGENCE AND SECURITY COMMITTEE
70 Whitehall London SW1A 2AS

On 7 July 2006 52 people were killed in the terrorist attacks in London. The Intelligence and Security Committee has examined the intelligence and security matters relevant to the attacks and I enclose with this letter a Report which covers our findings.

Investigations into the 7 and 21 July events continue, and therefore some information remains sub judice. As a result, and on the advice of the Law Officers in consultation with the Crown Prosecution Service, not all of the detail of which we are aware has been included. In laying the Report before Parliament you may wish to consult the Attorney General to assure yourself that the information it does contain will not prejudice current legal proceedings.

The Committee would be grateful if you could lay this Report before Parliament as soon as possible.

PAUL MURPHY

I'm quoting from Murphy's report and highlighted in bold the vital points. My added comments are in italics. And they were made as it was hot off the press in March 2006. The original is in front of me now. I find it even more distressing knowing so little has changed in the Scrooge-like attitude, the meanness, to dealing with the daily threats to lives.

The report says:

Fifty-two people were killed in the terrorist attacks in London on 7 July 2005 and several hundred were injured. We share the general horror and shock at this outrage and would like to take this opportunity to add our condolences to the families and friends of those killed, and sympathy to those injured, in these terrible attacks. We also extend our appreciation and gratitude to all those involved in the rescue and response effort.

The Attacks

1. On 7 July 2005 three explosions occurred at around 0850 on the London Underground system: the first on the Circle line between Aldgate and Liverpool Street, the next at Edgware Road station and the third on the Piccadilly line between Russell Square and King's Cross. At 0947 a fourth explosion occurred on the upper deck of a London bus in Tavistock Place. The bombers, who were also killed in what are known to have been suicide attacks, have been identified as: Mohammad Siddeque Khan, Hasib Hussein, Shazad Tanweer and Jermaine Lindsay. Investigations into these individuals and their associates are continuing.

2. On 21 July 2005 between 1235 and 1305 three incidents occurred on underground trains at or near Warren Street, Oval and Shepherd's Bush stations and one other on the upper deck of a bus in Hackney Road. These incidents, and the individuals allegedly involved, also remain under investigation.

3. On 11 July 2005 the Prime Minister made the following statement to Parliament on the 7 July bombings:

I would also like to say this about our police and intelligence services. I know of no intelligence specific enough to have allowed them to prevent last Thursday's attacks. By their very nature, people callous enough to kill completely innocent civilians in this way are hard to stop. But our services and police do a heroic job for our country day in, day out and I can say that over the past years, as this particular type of new and awful terrorist threat has grown, they have done their utmost to keep this country and its people safe. As I saw again from the meeting of COBR1[3] this morning, their determination to get those responsible is total.

The Report

4. On 13 July 2005 the Chairman of the Intelligence and Security Committee (ISC) wrote to the Prime Minister:

The Intelligence and Security Committee held its first meeting yesterday and has asked that I write to you. The Committee shares your revulsion at the murderous terrorist attacks last week and we commend the work undertaken by yourself, the emergency services and the Government to manage the situation... We fully endorse the current pri-

---

3   COBR is the term used within Government to refer to the high-level crisis management meetings, usually chaired by the Prime Minister, that are called when incidents such as the July terrorist attacks occur. The acronym COBR stands for Cabinet Office Briefing Room.

orities to prevent further attacks and to catch the perpetrators... as part of our oversight work, we plan to examine and take evidence on the intelligence and security matters surrounding the terrorist attacks in due course.

5. Various police investigations into the 7 and 21 July events continue and some matters remain sub judice, particularly in relation to the latter incidents. For this reason the Report does not consider the events of 21 July 2005, focusing instead on the 7 July attacks. Even so, given that investigations into the 7 July group are continuing, the picture of what is known, particularly about what happened in the run-up to those attacks, continues to change. This Report relates what is known and has been assessed at this point in time. It is possible that more information will come to light after this Report is published that will change that picture.

6. Our focus is the intelligence community and particularly the Security Service, the Secret Intelligence Service (SIS) and the Government Communications Headquarters (GCHQ). We have taken evidence from a number of witnesses including the heads of the security and intelligence Agencies. A detailed list is at Annex A. We have also examined a large number of Joint Intelligence Committee (JIC) and Joint Terrorism Analysis Centre (JTAC) intelligence assessments and other intelligence reports. In respect of their relationship with the Security Service,

we have also taken evidence from members of the police and received information from the Head of the Transport Security Team (TRANSEC) in the Department for Transport. **Given our remit, however, the Report does not seek to answer wider questions about the efficacy of the Government's counter-terrorist strategy and the adequacy or otherwise of the work being taken forward across a range of Government departments under this strategy. Nor do we seek to establish whether any of these wider policies (foreign and domestic) might have made a difference to preventing the July attacks.**

7. We note that a number of other bodies are covering issues relating to the 7 July attacks and that other reports will be published. The Home Office is producing an 'Official Account' of events: this was not available to the Committee prior to agreeing the Report.

8. **This Report sets out a number of conclusions and recommendations. These points should not overshadow the essential and excellent work the Agencies have undertaken against the terrorist threat in the UK. We record that ***4 terrorist plots in the UK have been thwarted by the intelligence and security Agencies since 11 September 2001, three of them since July 2005. Despite their successes disrupting these other plots, they did not manage to prevent**

---

4   Redacted

the attacks that took place in London on 7 July 2005.

9.   The Report refers in the main to 'Islamist terrorism'. This is the term used by the Security Service and the police to describe the current threat from individuals who claim a religious justification for terrorism, a claim which is rejected by most British Muslims, whose leaders point out that Islam is not a violent religion. **Across the wider Government counter-terrorism community the threat is also referred to as 'international terrorism' or 'AQ-related' terrorism.**

Aim and structure of the Report

10. The Report examines intelligence and security matters relevant to the July terrorist attacks and focuses in particular on:

- **Whether any intelligence which may have helped prevent the attacks was missed or overlooked.**
- **Why the threat level to the UK was lowered prior to the attacks and what impact this had; and what lessons were learned on the back of the attacks and how these are being applied, in particular:**
- **What reassessments of the threat have been made; and what is being done to increase coverage of the threat.**

SECTION 2: PRE-JULY CONTEXT
The Government's counter-terrorism strategy

11. Since 2002, Government work to counter Islamist terrorism has taken place under the Government's counter-terrorism strategy, known as CONTEST. This strategy has brought together the work of all departments (including that of the intelligence and security Agencies) under one aim: "to reduce the risk from international terrorism so that people can go about their business freely and with confidence".

12. The strategy divides work between that seeking to reduce the threat of an attack and that to reduce the UK's vulnerability to an attack. Reducing the threat includes work streams to PREVENT terrorism by reducing the number of individuals inspired to support Islamist terrorism or become terrorists, and work to PURSUE terrorists and those who assist them in order to disrupt potential attacks. Reducing vulnerability involves work streams to PROTECT potential targets (buildings, for example) in the UK and abroad and to PREPARE for the consequences of an attack through resilience and contingency planning. The overall work programme is referred to as the 'four P' framework.

How the intelligence and security Agencies contribute

13.   The Security Service, the SIS and GCHQ contribute to each of the four work streams as follows:

PREVENT – draws on Agency work on the causes of radicalisation for extremists and terrorists; PURSUE – involves Agency-led work on developing appropriate levels of capability to disrupt and bring to justice terrorist networks; PROTECT – encompasses the Agencies' work to provide protective security advice, from both physical and electronic attack; PREPARE – includes Agency input to risk assessments that underpin the resilience and response capabilities being developed.

I consider they failed in all four of those endeavours.

The four work streams encompass what the law dictates as a duty of care. If one is broken then negligence is evident, in this case all four were broken.

Counter-terrorist intelligence

14.   The acquisition of counter-terrorist intelligence by each of the three Agencies is critical to achieving success across each of these four strands and critical to the successful disruption of terrorist activity in the UK. The Security Service has primary responsibility under statute for the protection of national security against threats, including terrorism. The SIS and GCHQ support the Security Service in this

through the provision of intelligence from abroad. Intelligence on terrorist activity in the UK may come, for example, from communications between terrorists intercepted by GCHQ, from agents controlled by the SIS inside terrorist cells or networks overseas (connected back to the UK), from foreign liaison services, from physical surveillance by the Security Service or the police of terrorist or extremist activity in the UK, or from agents run by them within those networks in the UK.

15. Intelligence gathering in relation to CONTEST is driven through the JIC 'Requirements and Priorities' process. The JIC is the Committee of Agency heads and senior officials from Government departments responsible for providing Ministers and officials with intelligence assessments (known as JIC papers) on issues of national interest in the security, defence and foreign affairs fields. It is also responsible for the annual provision of a statement of the UK's Requirements and Priorities for secret intelligence collection, analysis and assessment. This statement sets out regional and thematic requirements under headings such as 'Islamist Terrorist Networks', 'Global Energy Markets and Security of Energy Supplies' and 'Weapons of Mass Destruction', which are then prioritised to reflect which issues are of greatest concern and which require the greatest intelligence effort. The **system currently has seven bands of priority, with**

Band 1 being the highest and Band 7 the lowest (for which intelligence will be collected on an 'opportunity only' basis).
What level was given to Khan as an imminent threat?

16. JTAC is the body that pulls together all the available intelligence on the Islamist threat, analyses it and produces short-term assessments of the level of threat and longer-term assessments of terrorist networks, capabilities and trends. JTAC was established in June 2003 as part of the Government's response to the growing terrorist threat. It is the only 'single issue' assessment body within the intelligence community.

The nature and limitations of intelligence

17. In previous reports the Committee has commented on the nature and limitations of intelligence. Secret intelligence is information which has to be obtained covertly rather than from open sources or diplomatic reporting. Lord Butler's Review of Intelligence on Weapons of Mass Destruction stated that:

The most important limitation on intelligence is its incompleteness. Much ingenuity and effort is spent on making secret information difficult to acquire and hard to analyse... it is often, when first acquired, sporadic and patchy, and even after analysis may still be at best inferential.

[Liaison services are foreign services which are in liaison with British intelligence and security services.]

18. In its 2003–2004 Annual Report this Committee noted that: The Agencies cannot know everything about everyone, nor can they intercept and read every communication **(which in any event would be a gross violation of human rights)**. There will always be gaps in the Agencies' knowledge.

Any consideration of whether or not the July bombings could have been prevented must bear these factors in mind.

19. The Director General of the Security Service [Dame Eliza Manningham-Buller] has said that intelligence rarely tells you all you want to know:

Often difficult decisions need to be made on the basis of intelligence which is fragmentary and difficult to interpret. In sum, some is gold, some dross and all of it requires validation, analysis and assessment. When it is gold it shines and illuminates, saves lives, protects nations and informs policy. When identified as dross it needs to be rejected: that may take some confidence. At the end of the day, it requires people of integrity not only to collect it but also to prioritise, sift, judge and use it.

Security Service investigations

20. An investigation is the process by which intelligence collection resources and analysis are directed to develop these fragmentary pieces of information into

a picture of activity, identity, intentions and location. The picture that emerges is rarely complete and the investigative process then involves seeking further information and analysis, to make the picture clearer.

21. The volume of intelligence received on terrorist activity can be overwhelming, and difficult decisions have to be made as to what priority to accord a particular piece of intelligence and whether that piece or another lead should be pursued in more depth. Intensive 'round the clock' coverage of a single target can require up to *** Security Service surveillance staff out of a total of around *** surveillance staff, and around *** organisation staff. An intensive operation, for example into imminent attack planning, can consume almost half of the Security Service's operational and investigative resources. Intelligence officers therefore have to make difficult professional judgements as to where finite resources should be allocated and focus on those targets that appear to pose the most immediate threat to life.

22. In 2001, at around the time of 9/11, the Security Service knew of approximately 250 primary investigative targets in the UK. By July 2004 this had risen to over 500, of which only about *** could be investigated, and only *** intensively. By July 2005 the number of primary investigative targets in the UK had risen to around 800, only about *** % of which the Service was able to cover. Even then the degree

of coverage on the most essential subjects was far from complete.

23. In order to help prioritise investigative effort, assessments are made as to what category targets fall into. Prior to July these categories were 'Essential', 'Desirable' and 'Other':

Essential – an individual who is likely to be directly involved in, or have knowledge of, plans for terrorist activity, or an individual who may have knowledge of terrorist activity;

Desirable – an individual who is associated with individuals who are directly involved in, or have knowledge of, plans for terrorist activity or who is raising money for terrorism or who is in jail and would be an essential target if at large.

Khan was in both these categories.

Other – an individual who may be associated with individuals who are directly involved in, or have knowledge of, plans for terrorist activity.

24. **The Security Service works in the UK with the police to develop its investigations leading to disruptions of plots, arrests and convictions. In making investigative decisions the Security Service recognises, partly because of the resources available, that it has to be selective and that it has to bear risks. Proportionality is also taken into account in the decision-making process: consideration is given to what degree of intrusion is proportionate on the basis**

of the available intelligence. Targets move between investigative tiers as new information of activities and intentions is received, and cases and priorities are regularly reviewed to ensure that resources are appropriately allocated.

Back to these resources again – whose responsibility is it?

The threat from Islamist terrorism prior to July

25. **Prior to July 2005 UK interests had been targeted successfully by Islamist terrorists, most notably in November 2003 in the Al Qaida-associated car bomb attack on the British Consulate and HSBC in Istanbul. British citizens had also been the victims of Islamist terrorist attacks in the United States on 11 September 2001, Bali on 12 October 2002 and Madrid on 11 March 2004. The bombings on 7 July 2005 were the first successful Islamist terrorist attacks in the UK.**

This does not exonerate anyone of the lack of intelligence in regards to 7/7.

26. Since 9/11 the Government and the intelligence and security Agencies have continued to warn of the high level of threat to the UK from Islamist terrorism. In a speech in his Sedgefield constituency on 5 March 2004, the Prime Minister warned of the continuing global threat from terrorism. He said: It is monstrously premature to think the threat has passed. The

risk remains in the balance here and abroad. These days decisions about it come thick and fast, and while they are not always of the same magnitude they are hardly trivial. Let me give you an example. A short while ago, during the war, we received specific intelligence warning of a major attack on Heathrow.

27. **On 6 August 2004 the Home Secretary issued a statement on the terrorist threat to the UK in which he said: I have made clear repeatedly that there is a continuing threat to the UK, which has remained high for some time. We are maintaining a state of readiness and taking every feasible precautionary measure to protect British citizens, both here and abroad, consistent with the level of threat.** *Too little – too late.*

28. At around the same time the Security Service website warned:

The most significant threat to the UK and to UK interests overseas comes from Al Qaida and associated networks. The threat to the UK remains real and serious... **We know that both British and foreign nationals belonging to 9 cells and associated networks are currently present throughout the UK, that they are supporting the activities of terrorist groups, and that in some cases they are engaged in planning, or attempting to carry out, terrorist attacks.**

But they insist Khan had no links to Al Qaida.

29. The possibility that attacks could be being planned without detection by the Agencies had been acknowl-

edged prior to July. The previous Metropolitan Police Commissioner [Lord Stevens] was widely reported to believe that it was not a matter of 'if' an attack would occur, but 'when'. In 2003, the Director General of the Security Service warned that: ... the nature of counter-terrorism is to get ahead of the game to stop, frustrate or otherwise prevent terrorist activity. That is the primary goal but the reality is that we can never stop all such attacks and no security intelligence organisation in the world could do so. **An attack may get through our defences...**

Even more so if the defences are not resourced.

30. As attacks against the UK have been mounted and successfully disrupted in the period since 9/11, the intelligence community's understanding of the scale of the threat against the UK has advanced. The Chief of the Assessments Staff told the Committee:

I think the more we learned over this period of several years, the more we began to realise the limits of what we knew, and I think that remains the case.

The fear of unidentified attack planning intensified following the attacks in Madrid in March 2004 as they showed that terrorist networks could engage in unseen operational activity despite even intensive investigative efforts. In June 2005 the JIC judged that Western states could not be confident of identifying preparations for attacks, and that there would probably be a successful attack of some sort in the UK in the next five years.

This is what infuriates me for it seems obvious that more stringent checks of possible threats were and are needed and in our significantly perilous world more resources are required by the Security Services. My questions then: Where are the resources coming from? How can we make it possible to efficiently carry out the checks? There are still no answers as far as I can see. One other question that still bugs me – how much information was used to compile the following section of the report?

SECTION 3: THE 7 JULY ATTACKS: WAS ANY INTELLIGENCE MISSED OR OVERLOOKED?

31. Against this background the Committee has taken detailed evidence on what was known about the attackers and the plans for an attack prior to 7 July 2005, with a view in particular to identifying whether anything was missed or overlooked by the Agencies which might have prevented the attacks. Not all of the detail of which we are aware can be included at this time for legal reasons.

32. We have not sought to investigate in detail (though we set out some background below) who the group were, how they became radicalised, or how they planned and executed the attacks. This goes beyond our remit to cover the work of the intelligence and security Agencies and, in this context, what they knew about the 7 July group. We understand that these areas

will be covered in more detail by the Home Office's 'Official Account', announced by the Home Secretary in December 2005.

Background

33. The 7 July bombers have been identified as Mohammed Siddeque Khan (30), Hasib Hussein (18), Shazad Tanweer (22), and Jermaine Lindsay (19). All apart from Jermaine Lindsay were British nationals of Pakistani origin, born and brought up in the UK, and at the time of the bombings based in West Yorkshire. Lindsay was a British national of West Indian origin, born in Jamaica and based in Aylesbury prior to the attacks. He was a convert to Islam.

34. On the day of the attacks the group assembled at Luton train station and travelled together to King's Cross from where they dispersed to conduct their near simultaneous explosions. The first three explosions took place at around 0850 but the fourth device was not detonated until over an hour later. **The fourth bomber, Hasib Hussin, stopped to buy batteries before boarding the bus – it is possible that this indicates he had difficulty setting off his device.**

35. Post-incident forensic analysis has shown that the explosions were caused by **home-made organic peroxide-based devices,** packed into rucksacks. Organic peroxide explosive is dangerous to manufac-

ture because of its instability but it does not require a great deal of expertise and can be made using readily available materials and domestic equipment. The devices were almost certainly detonated manually by the bombers themselves in intentional suicide attacks. **Some small home-made devices were left in the car at Luton railway station** although the reason for this is unclear. There is no apparent significance in the choice of 7 July as the date for the attacks and no indication that the G8 conference which was taking place at Gleneagles, Scotland at the time was a factor.

36. Investigations since July have shown that the group was in contact with others involved in extremism in the UK, including a number of people who *** . **There is no intelligence to indicate that there was a fifth or further bombers.**

37. Siddeque Khan is now known to have visited Pakistan in 2003 and to have spent several months there with Shazad Tanweer between November 2004 and February 2005. It has not yet been established who they met in Pakistan, **but it is assessed as likely that they had some contact with Al Qaida figures.**

38. The extent to which the 7 July attacks were externally planned, directed or controlled by contacts in Pakistan or elsewhere remains unclear. The Agencies believe that some form of operational training is likely to have taken place while Khan and Tanweer were in Pakistan. Contacts in the run-up to the

attacks suggest they may have had advice or direction from individuals there. **Claims in the media that a 'mastermind' left the UK the day before the attacks reflect one strand of an investigation that was subsequently discounted by the intelligence and security Agencies.**

39. Since the attacks, various claims of responsibility have been made. Shortly afterwards a letter was posted on the internet claiming that the attacks were conducted by the 'Secret Organisation of al-Qaida in Europe'. This claim was not assessed to be credible by the Agencies. On 1 September 2005 a video message from Siddeque Khan was aired on Al Jazeera in which he said: I and thousands like me are forsaking everything for what we believe. Our driving motivation doesn't come from tangible commodities that this world has to offer. Our religion is Islam – obedience to the one true God, Allah, and following the footsteps of the final prophet and messenger Muhammad... Your democratically elected Governments continuously perpetuate atrocities against my people all over the world. And your support of them makes you directly responsible, just as I am directly responsible for protecting and avenging my Muslim brothers and sisters. Until we feel security, you will be our targets. And until you stop the bombing, gassing, imprisonment and torture of my people we will not stop this fight. We are at war and I am a soldier.

40. The video message went on to praise Osama Bin Laden and Ayman al-Zawaheri as heroes, although no indication was given that the attacks had been directed by them. Ayman al-Zawaheri appeared on the same tape in a separate recording and praised the 'blessed battle' which had transferred to the 'enemy's land'. In a later videotaped message, aired on Al Jazeera on 19 September, al-Zawaheri claimed responsibility for the attacks. We have been told by the Agencies that this claim is not supported by any firm evidence. **The degree of Al Qaida involvement both in terms of support and control remains under investigation.**

41. Documents recovered from the scenes of the attacks on 7 July gave an indication of the possible identities of the four men involved. Once these were confirmed, the Security Service and the other Agencies initiated reviews of their records to establish whether they had come across any of the individuals before 7 July, whether they had had any prior intelligence of the attacks, or whether the attacks made the meaning of any existing intelligence clearer.

42. Due to sub judice rules this Report does not cover the 21 July events in detail. We can, however, report that the Agencies currently **have no evidence of direct links between the 7 July attacks and those involved and the incidents on 21 July.**

43. We have been told in evidence that none of the individuals involved in the 7 July group had been identi-

fied (that is, named and listed) as potential terrorist threats prior to July. We have also been told that there was no warning from intelligence (including foreign intelligence) of the plans to attack the London transport network on 7 July 2005.

Plans for an attack

44. There was much media speculation following the attacks and various claims were made that prior warning had been given. We have been assured by the Agencies that there was no prior warning of the attacks that took place from any source, including from foreign intelligence services. We have looked in detail into claims that the Saudi Arabian authorities warned the British Agencies about the attacks. **We found that some information was passed to the Agencies about possible terrorist planning for an attack in the UK. It was examined by the Agencies who concluded that the plan was not credible.** That information has been given to us: it is materially different from what actually occurred on 7 July and clearly not relevant to these attacks.

45. Having reviewed its records once details of the bombers came to light, the Security Service did find, however, that it had come across two members of the 7 July group before on the peripheries of other investigations. These were Siddeque Khan and Shazad

Tanweer. GCHQ and SIS had not come across any members of the group.

46. In the comprehensive review of intelligence records that it conducted, **the Security Service found that it had on record a telephone number which it was only possible to identify after the attacks as belonging to Jermaine Lindsay. They also had on record a telephone number registered to a 'Siddeque Khan' and details of contacts between that number and an individual who had been under Security Service investigation in 2003.** A review of related surveillance data showed that Siddeque Khan and Shazad Tanweer had been among a group of men who had held meetings with others under Security Service investigation in 2004.

47. We asked the Security Service whether, having looked back at the intelligence that existed, more attention should have been paid to Siddeque Khan and Shazad Tanweer at the time, or whether there were any clues about their future intentions to conduct terrorist attacks. In relation to the contacts in 2003, the Security Service said it was apparent that meetings were being planned but that there was no information as to the purpose of the proposed meetings. There was (and still is) no evidence that they were connected to planning terrorist acts. The individual under investigation was not himself an 'Essential' target and there was no reason for his contacts, which we now know

to have been with Siddeque Khan, to have been identified as exceptional or worthy of further investigation above other priorities.

48. As for the meetings in 2004, we found that they were covered by the Security Service as part of an important and substantial ongoing investigation. Siddeque Khan and Shazad Tanweer were among a number of unidentified men at the meetings. The Security Service did not seek to investigate or identify them at the time although we have been told that it would probably have been possible to do so had the decision been taken. The judgement was made (correctly with hindsight) that they were peripheral to the main investigation and there was no intelligence to suggest they were interested in planning an attack against the UK. Intelligence at the time suggested that their focus was training and insurgency operations in Pakistan and schemes to defraud financial institutions. As such, there was no reason to divert resources away from other higher priorities, which included investigations into attack planning against the UK.

49. **Once resources became available, an investigation was launched by the Security Service into over *** unidentified contacts who had come to light on the periphery of the earlier (2004) investigation. This included, among others, the unidentified men who we now know to have been Siddeque Khan and Shazad Tanweer. However, resources were**

soon diverted again to higher priorities. Further attempts were made to return to the men involved in the meetings in 2004 as resources became available. Some of them were subsequently identified and categorised as 'Essential', 'Desirable' or 'Other' targets and more intensive investigations were conducted. Only limited additional attempts were made to identify the men we now know to have been Siddeque Khan and Shazad Tanweer, and to find out more about their activities. They were not categorised as investigative targets because, on the basis of the available intelligence, there was no reason to suggest they should be investigated above other more pressing priorities at the time.

50. It has become clear since 7 July that Siddeque Khan was also referred to in reporting by detainees (from outside the UK) in early 2004. This reporting referred to men from the UK known only by pseudonyms who had travelled to Pakistan in 2003 and sought meetings with Al Qaida figures. The Security Service sought at the time to establish the true identities of the men but without success. In the aftermath of the 7 July attacks, Siddeque Khan was identified by one of the detainees (having seen a press photograph) as one of the men referred to in the detainee reporting. It is now known that Siddeque Khan travelled to Pakistan in 2003 and spent time there with Shazad Tanweer from November 2004 to February 2005.

51. We have been told that as part of the investigation into the unidentified men at the meetings mentioned earlier (paragraph 49) photographs were circulated to some foreign intelligence services and foreign detaining authorities in an attempt to see if anything more about the individuals was known. A photograph of Siddeque Khan was shown to one of the detainees who had provided the earlier information, but without positive result.

52. As far as the Security Service is able to tell from records to date, this photograph was not sent or shown to the detainee who later identified Siddeque Khan. Had it been, and had the detainee been able to identify Khan as one of the subjects of the earlier report, it is possible that the Security Service might have allocated more effort to identifying and investigating him prior to July. While this was a missed opportunity, there is no guarantee that the detainee would have identified him from the photograph, particularly given its very poor quality. There is also no guarantee that had the detainee identified him significantly greater resources would have been put into pursuing him, particularly given the other investigative priorities around at that time, which included the disruption of known plots to attack the UK.

53. **A report from another source has also recently come to light. This report was passed to the Security Service in February 2005. It stated that a man**

named '***' had travelled to Afghanistan in the late 1990s/early 2000s with another man named 'Imran' and that both held extremist views. The Security Service and police undertook some further investigation into the two men at the time, without significant result. After the 7 July attacks the source identified '***' as Siddeque Khan.

54. It has become clear since the July attacks that Siddeque Khan was the subject of reporting of which the Security Service was aware prior to July 2005. However, his true identity was not revealed in this reporting and it was only after the 7 July attacks that the Security Service was able to identify Khan as the subject of the reports.

55. **It is also clear that, prior to the 7 July attacks, the Security Service had come across Siddeque Khan and Shazad Tanweer on the peripheries of other surveillance and investigative operations. At that time their identities were unknown to the Security Service and there was no appreciation of their subsequent significance. As there were more pressing priorities at the time, including the need to disrupt known plans to attack the UK, it was decided not to investigate them further or seek to identify them. When resources became available, attempts were made to find out more about these two and other peripheral contacts, but these resources were soon diverted back to what were considered to be higher investigative priorities.**

56. **It is possible that the chances of identifying attack**

planning and of preventing the 7 July attacks might have been greater had different investigative decisions been taken in 2003–2005. Nonetheless, we conclude that, in light of the other priority investigations being conducted and the limitations on Security Service resources, the decisions not to give greater investigative priority to these two individuals were understandable.

57. In reaching this conclusion we have been struck by the sheer scale of the problem that our intelligence and security Agencies face and their comparatively small capacity to cover it. The Agencies had to reassess their capacity to cope as a result of the July attacks – an issue that we will consider in more detail in Sections 5 and 6.[5]

****

I've included much of their full report because I think it is so vitally important that you know what they found – or were willing to officially publish – and where we are today. More than a quarter of the way through the 21st Century and I don't believe we are ready for another 7/7. Either to deal with such an atrocity or to look after survivors. That can't be right. What I would have liked, as some sort of acceptance of calamity, was for Sir John Scarlett as head of MI5 five to

---

5   The Intelligence and Security Committee Report into the London Terrorist Attacks on 7 July 2005 quoted by Dan Biddle was presented to Parliament in May 2006 and is designated © Crown Copyright 2006 and extracts are published with that official arrangement.

invite me to a closed-door meeting, sit me down and say: 'Mr. Biddle, we are terribly sorry we got it wrong, and we are terribly sorry for the impact this has had on you.' Of course, I haven't, because nobody within MI5 has ever been held accountable for those failures. We were collateral damage.

They absolutely knew what Khan and his guys were going to do, and they did nothing. And then I'm living my life in a way that's totally alien to me, in a body that I still don't recognise and doesn't feel or react like it's my body. And out there are these Government spy people in their offices doing the same things they were doing 20 years ago. Life hasn't changed for them. Yet my life will never be what it was, and I live with the emotional and mental trauma of that day every day. There ain't a day goes by where I don't see Khan's face in the flashback of memory. It's like being haunted by a man that never was. Officially.

While the troubling years went on, and life never seemed to get any easier, I made fragile and fleeting contact with the woman who would be my saviour. If it was happenstance that put me on that Tube carriage just beyond Edgware Road on 7/7, and my goodness with the events of that day, it was against the odds, what brought Gem into my life? Kismet? Fate? What can you call it?

Strange as this may sound it was my bloody good luck, the treasure I take away from being blown to bits. Of course, I must explain, after I fell in love, I tried to kill myself three times. That's why they call it Complex Post Traumatic Stress.

PART THREE
LOVE AND OTHER HAZARDS

'Homo sum, humani nihil a me alienum puto; I am a human, and so nothing human is alien to me.'
– ROMAN PLAYWRIGHT TERENCE, 166 BC

Chapter Ten

LOVE HURTS

*'Doubt is an unpleasant condition, but certainty is
an absurd one.'*
— VOLTAIRE, 1768.

WHAT IF? THAT'S SURELY the question of my life.

Lots of spirited victims fought for life that day, that 7/7 in 2005, but their hearts stopped. Yet mine beats on and each day has been a lesson in living. And understanding, to some degree, the events and perpetrators of that day's atrocity simmering in tandem with my outrage at all the political promises and vacuous talk and grand gestures which point to solutions but go nowhere.

I repeat, what if? For I believe I live on today because of a random and wrongly sent Facebook friend request. It was from a woman called Gem who turned out to be just that. And my saviour. Her request was intended for a friend's son who was also called Daniel. Rushing off to work, she clicked on the wrong Dan. I was sitting in the bungalow in Essex when my phone pinged, and I looked at the picture of the sender. I didn't hesitate to accept. And that was that – for four years. We didn't talk, simply followed our lives through Facebook posts. I was still trying to find myself and was plagued every day by visits from Khan and through the night by the horrors of the tunnel. I didn't feel like *chatting*.

It was an introverted time for me, probably my most troubling period since 7/7. Nothing seemed to go smoothly. I'd find myself in a job I liked but then be plagued by Complex PTSD and only just be able to live with myself and the terrors, never mind work. During this weary period, I received a letter on 30 July 2010 formally requesting I give evidence at the Coroner's Inquest into 7/7 being held by Lady Justice Hallett at the Royal Courts of Justice on 11 October 2010. Indeed, Dame Heather was making it clear she *expected* me to give evidence. That's because I'd kicked off when the police first told me the inquest was upcoming. I so much wanted a public inquiry – not this rehash of events.

I refused at first to attend and give evidence. The inquest, officially, was to ascertain the place of death, time of death, cause of death and the perpetrator. *We knew all that.* To put people through absolute torment again didn't make sense to me. I told the police liaison officer and her team when I met them that I wouldn't go, and she said: 'There's probably something that's going to make you feel even more strongly about not coming – the mayor has invited the families of the bombers to attend the inquest.'

I was thankful to London Mayor Ken Livingstone, who had been helpful to my family, gone beyond what he had to, while I was in hospital, but he'd invited the bombers' family, including Khan's wife, to the inquest? Ken Livingstone was a good guy in all this – I've no fucking time for Tony Blair and John Reid – but this was going too far. I told the liaison in front of four Old Bill:

'If you make me come to this and she's within ten feet of me I'll kill her so the next trial you have will be mine. I'm not joking. I'll kill her.'

All the coppers kind of stepped back at that, and she went: 'I understand you're angry.'

I told her: 'You can never fucking understand the anger.'

I said that it was an insult not only to me, but to the families of people that lost someone. Khan was not a victim in this; he didn't deserve to be mentioned. I was livid and threatening and repeated that if his wife turned up it would be the last fucking place she ever visited. The wife refused to go in the end. My anger was overwhelming.

I took legal advice about suing the bombers' families but that was a non-starter. Could I sue the Government? Yes, but if I lost, I'd be liable for possibly hundreds of thousands of pounds in costs. I looked at the lawyer and asked: 'What you're saying is, I've been shafted all ends up and I've got no recourse whatsoever. I've just got to basically suck it up.'

She gave me a weak smile: 'To be blunt, yes.'

I had to give evidence at the inquest. It was probably one of the most emotionally challenging things I've ever gone through. When it was my turn (there were 309 witnesses in court and 19 other interviews) I was explicit about my experience in the tunnel. About the attack, the aftermath, my rescue and most of all of the encompassing horror of it all. I didn't need notes. I didn't need my memory prompted. I spoke from the script in my head – the script that precisely matches the movie of the events that's on a loop in my brain. I sensed nervous coughs and that movement of people when it's not their bodies that are uncomfortable but their minds. It's a contagious, silent shuffle.

One of the barristers quizzed me on my statement, which was 60 pages long, and about being pinned down by the metal work and I attempted to explain how otherworldly it was being in this twilight zone of not knowing if I was alive or dead. I talked about trying to move the train doors off my legs and something digging in my back. The barrister asked:

'What was it?'

I knew very well but had held back the image, freeze-framed in my memory:

'A black brogue shoe with a foot with a purple, red and gold Pringle sock on it.'

With that, a woman in the public gallery screamed. It was part of her dead husband I was talking about. She'd bought him the Pringle socks for Christmas. It makes me shiver now. I was causing that woman so much pain for something that we all knew the answers to. When you suffer from survivor's guilt and then you do that, are responsible for more pain, it's devastating.

When I got out of the witness box, I lost it. I managed to get myself settled in the next-door waiting room, but I was inconsolable for about an hour. I couldn't get my head around what I had put a victim's family through. I was angry with myself, frustrated – and frightened of the years ahead, for the future. Would anyone ever understand?

The inquest emphasised for me the futility of that question. Officialdom doesn't see the human side. That irks survivors like me. Khan flicked a switch and that did it. I badgered all the medical people asking if he hurt when he did that. They told me his brain wouldn't have had time to register pain, the explosion would decimate him too quickly. That angers me – at least suffer. My idea would have been that he was blown to bits – and lived on in absolute agony for the rest of his life. There's a lot whizzing about in your head when you sit there thinking all these people lost their lives and 982 suffered untold horrors and injuries for something that was blatantly obviously going to happen. The 'learn lessons' brigade helps no one.

The inquest, despite the professional and empathetic Dame Heather, wasn't a substitute for a public inquiry which I and many survivors and families of victims campaigned for. But very cleverly, the Government went for an inquest. We'd launched proceedings in 2007 to seek a judicial review of the decision by the then Home Secretary, John Reid, not to hold a public inquiry. Reid argued that such an inquiry would require 'a pretty massive reallocation of resources... away from those needing protection at a critical time'. The proceedings were stayed – and that held – pending the conclusion of the inquest. People don't differentiate between an inquest and a public inquiry, and I was congratulated: 'Great, brilliant, you've got your inquiry.'

We hadn't. I knew an inquest wouldn't give me the answers I wanted. It wasn't going to trace back how much the intelligence services knew about Khan and the damning evidence they had of a fermenting conspiracy. It was a nonsense and the get out of jail card was always 'security' – can't tell you that because of 'national security'.

It was a protective shield for any difficult questions about what had really gone on, what the spooks truly knew about the bombers before they triggered their personal contribution to Armageddon; an inquest was a way of defending the mishaps of British Intelligence. Remember, the defence MI6 put forward at the inquest was they knew Khan and his gang posed an imminent threat, but they believed the imminent threat would be on foreign soil not in the UK; that they were planning a terrorist attack in another country. 'And therefore, didn't warrant the expenditure for surveillance in the UK...'

The inquest conclusions, after 19 weeks of evidence, had some bite but I felt it was with false teeth. In her conclusions, Dame Heather criticised lapses by emergency services and by MI5. She picked up on one incident, a moment in the whole business but so very, very crucial. She said MI5 should review its procedures on showing photographs to informants. She concluded: 'The security services failed to show a colour surveillance photograph of two of the bombers (Khan and Shehzad Tanweer) to an al-Qaeda supergrass before the attacks. The photo was cut in half and cropped by an MI5 desk officer who, it was said (in inquest evidence), "must have been very busy or acting at great speed".

She said MI5's chief of staff – who gave evidence as 'Witness G' – had 'speculated' that the cropped photograph of Khan was of such poor quality that it was not deemed worth showing and added: 'This, of course, begs the question of why the photographs were cropped in this way. They were dreadful.' She said she was troubled by Witness G's evidence that it was not normal practice for photos to be revisited when new sources became available.

She criticised MI5's record-keeping: 'Witness G himself had to visit retired desk officers at their homes to discover as best he could what they had done and why. I fully expect the Security Service to review their procedures to ensure that good quality images are shown and that whatever went wrong on this occasion does not happen again.' She called for better communication and sharing of information about terrorist subjects between MI5 and the police.

What I thought most damning – and still do – was Dame Heather's chastisement of the spooks. As I explained before, there was some bite.

She criticised MI5, saying she did not accept that the Security Service had made every possible improvement since 7/7. During the inquest the aforementioned Witness G, and James Eadie QC, counsel for the Home Secretary and MI5, argued the agency had learned from its mistakes. Dame Hallett said: 'I feel unable to accept Mr Eadie and Witness G's assurances that all is now well within the security services.'

I think all of us who went through 7/7 were glad of the verdict of unlawful killing but most of us wanted the inquiry we never got. Most importantly, I think, for everyone was the highlighting of MI5's 2004 questionable assessment that Khan and Tanweer were not a threat to national security. Yet, a future Prime Minister, Theresa May, who as the Home Secretary when the inquest concluded in May 2011, held the political line of being 'pleased that the coroner has made clear there is simply no evidence that the Security Service knew of, and therefore failed to prevent, the bombings on 7/7. We are always looking to learn lessons and to improve the response to the terrorist threat we face'.

Yeah, 'lessons to be learned', etc, etc, etc… it was not a popular view. Let's allow some others to have their say. Marie Fatayi-Williams, whose 26-year-old son Anthony died at Tavistock Square, said only a public inquiry could address concerns about the Security Service. David Foulkes' dad Graham vainly called for an independent inquiry with 'a much broader scope and a much broader remit' than the inquest.

For the victims' families and survivors, none of this

was cathartic. We waited five years for the inquest. Ros Morley, whose husband, Colin, was killed in the Edgware Road bombing, spoke for a lot of us: 'Over the past year the process itself has been mentally and emotionally tiring and at times, utterly exhausting. It is to be hoped that this includes great improvements to the security services.'

Ben Thwaites, who like me survived Edgware Road, said: 'It would appear that official lines have now, after much resistance, been closed to us. I feel that there are actions that could have been taken to protect others and truths that could have been shared that have been brushed aside. I can only hope that this does not lead to unnecessary loss of life in the future.'

Ben was more optimistic than me. I was, and remain, appalled at Tony Blair's Government's handling of 7/7, the sanctimony and the running from questions. The inquest confirmed my feelings. The bombings were dealt with like *it's an absolute national tragedy but let's just try and brush it under the carpet as quick as we can.* I think it was because of the failure of the Security Services.

As I've said many times before, if everybody had been killed, I can't help believing the explanation offered could have been three electrical faults and an engine explosion; no witnesses and it could have been covered up. The horror of the events portrayed the Government in such a bad light and everything that went on after just emphasised what a bunch they were.

Like the memorial service in November 2005 at St Paul's

Cathedral; window dressing around deadly errors of judgment.

The casual indifference of our so-called leaders persists. That buffoon Boris Johnson writes in his mistake-riddled book *Unleashed*, published in October 2024, that 36 people were killed on 7/7. One book reviewer, Leo Robson, pointed out the true figure and called Johnson's slapdash treatment 'an especially sad and weird error in a book that devotes 120 pages to what (in Johnson's verdict) a stupendous Mayor of London he became'.

Such shite coming from a pathetic person like Johnson doesn't sting as much as the nonsense from others who should know better. But it hurts nevertheless and can set things off. Tim O'Toole, who was the Managing Director of London Underground (he quit in 2009 when Johnson was mayor) was the only official who said sorry to me. He visited me at Roehampton and said: 'I'm so sorry that this happened to you on a service that we provide.' He was the only one. Many Muslim doctors and nurses sympathised with and spoke some genuine words that helped. But Tim O'Toole, yes, the only official. Sir John Scarlett of MI5 never did – how could he? Nobody within MI5 has ever been held accountable for the failures around 7/7.

The powers that be certainly displayed no understanding of the hidden horrors that follow such atrocities. Of mis-speaking and misinterpreting. The terrors are hidden if hauntingly familiar, like day and night, to the victims.

I knew I needed help from the start. When I was in St

Mary's Hospital there was a psychologist who spoke to me, but when you suffer the level of trauma that I did, it takes a very specific skill set and a very specific understanding of what somebody goes through, and he just didn't have it. It's not a criticism of him, it wasn't his forte.

I'm not a religious individual whatsoever, but the hospital pastor always used to come by and have a cup of tea. We didn't talk religion. It was nothing like that. We'd chat and I'd kind of explain how I was feeling. He was quite beneficial, more so than the psychologist who was trying to get me to reframe my thinking, and my brain wasn't in a position to do that, I was still trying to work out how the fuck this had happened. To simply talk to somebody who listened, and let me go at my own pace, was great, reviving.

When I went to Roehampton, where I was waking the ward up screaming with night terrors, they assigned another psychologist to me. She tried to get me to do cognitive behavioural therapy, a talking therapy, and that was not what I needed. The psychologist announced one day that we were going to do empty chair therapy. It was like going to the circus.

She told me I had to imagine a chair in the corner of the room and sitting in it was 'the person who did this to you'. She wanted me to 'see' Khan, who I was already encountering too many fucking times a day for my sanity. She asked: 'What would you say to him?'

And I said: 'Nothing.'

'What do you mean nothing?'

'I'd say nothing.'

'But what would you do?'

'I'd smash his fucking head in with my crutches.'

'Well, I wasn't expecting that. You wouldn't say anything?'

'There are no words. You can't talk to somebody like that. For me, you meet that person with the same actions that they met you with. I'd smash his fucking head in until his brains were over the wall.'

'That's not going to work...'

I don't think she liked that too much. I've had people turn around and say to me, 'I think it's time you forgave the bomber', and I think: *It's time you fucking get away from me, because otherwise you'll be the person who needs a wheelchair next.*

I think this is the avenue that psychologists tried to get me to go down, to find that piece of me that can forgive and enable me to move on.

I am very open about this. I detest Khan with every fibre of my being but it's not all-consuming, I don't live every day with him fixated in my brain. There's just a part of me that thinks if he wasn't dead, I'd kill him myself. It's that simple, but that doesn't dictate the way I live my life. That doesn't dictate the things I do. It's just a part of me that burns strongly, that I would love to rip him apart with my bare hands.

One of the things that really frustrates me about forgiveness is if you forgive somebody, they need to be looking for your forgiveness, and those bastards would never do that. And if Khan hadn't died, I believe he would have gone on to do it again. This wasn't a case of somebody nicking a few penny sweets out at the corner shop. This was four individuals who killed 52 people and maimed and injured hundreds more.

And people are telling me, you should forgive it. It's almost like saying, well, let's just put them on probation and they'll learn from that. They'll learn the error of their ways. I've never understood this whole thing when people whose sons and daughters have been raped or murdered stand outside a court saying they forgive the bad bastard who did it. Do they think the asshole who has been locked up gives two shits if they forgive him or not? Because if he cared that much, he wouldn't have done it in the first place. There's moving on but importantly there's moving on and not forgetting or forgiving evil.

There are things in life that are so big, so damaging, I find it difficult to comprehend. The enormity and the ripples from 7/7 go far beyond those of us that were on the trains and buses that day. But I think when I look at 7/7 and then look at other atrocities that have happened since in the UK, 7/7 rarely gets mentioned on the anniversaries. The Government would rather it went away.

The memorial in Hyde Park is 52 stainless steel columns that stick out the ground. It's fucking horrible. Manchester got a beautiful memorial garden after the Ariana Grande concert bombings. It is somewhere families can go to reflect, do whatever they need to do. It's a beautiful, serene place. We got 52 metal poles sticking out of the ground. How does that represent 52 lost lives? I think the whole attitude towards 7/7 by the Government has been disgraceful, when it happened, and everything afterwards. I have all of these things going through me, and when I think back to the more immediate aftermath and to that psychologist asking me what I'd do if Khan was sitting in the corner. What *did* she expect me to say?

I found I just had to get on with it, trying to contain the emotion, control, if possible, the impact of Complex Post Traumatic Stress and carry on being alive. Which I now know would have been impossible without Gem and that accidental connection via Facebook.

Chapter Eleven

HIGH MAINTENANCE

'One daffodil is worth a thousand pleasures.'
– WILLIAM WORDSWORTH, I WANDERED LONELY AS A
CLOUD, 1807

THE FRIENDSHIP BEGAN BY exchanging messages, the romance with us sharing nightmares.

Gem and I had been Facebook acquaintances for four years, a time of huge personal difficulty for me, a time when I so often wished I'd not been carried out of the tunnel at Edgware Road, when I had no peripheral visions, I was staring ahead into an abyss. Work, when I wasn't attacked by PTSD, when I'd exorcised Khan and the gang from my head, was a welcome respite.

In 2013, I was working for Hilton, assessing accessibility at their hotels, and on my lunch break I was sifting through the internet. I was puzzling over some snag with a ramp access to a property and truly not paying that much attention to what was buzzing up on my screen. Then, there she was – Gem. A friend had a nasty fall, and Gem had mentioned it on Facebook, and I sent a goodwill message. Just a note and we had a couple of friendly interactions after that. A few weeks later she was having a package of problems, and we started regularly messaging, chatting as it were.

For me, it was nice to have someone to 'talk' to. For so long I'd felt no one in the world was listening to me.

It turned out we both have an acquired sort of humour. We shared some silly messages with her having a go at me for being a stereotypical London lad and me retaliating about her being Welsh and besotted by daffodils. Silly stuff between a couple of people who were finding ways to connect. And, for me, there were no awkward moments. Of course, we hadn't met – Gem could have been messaging from Australia. Gem never knew me in any way other than as a physically damaged man. She was talking with me as I forever am, not who I was. For me, that was real. We kept on 'talking' and I knew I had feelings for her that were more than just being 'pen pals'. I was frightened of that – we'd never met. Might I spoil it? And I was apprehensive about my loving feelings. Was I still entitled to have any?

I was even more emotionally attached after we began speaking on the phone. They were long calls, and sometimes quite intense conversations. Gem was the first person I told my 7/7 story to in its entirety; from start to finish, she never said a word. She listened. I unloaded my whole experience. Most people feel obliged to say, 'Oh, yeah, I know how you feel', or some such, but she didn't. She let me talk. She didn't interrupt at all. We didn't know each other very well so I'm opening up to a stranger; at no point was she glibly muttering 'I know how you feel', and 'I understand'. She *listened* and nobody had done that, done what I so desperately needed. I knew that she was somebody very special and she was the person that I wanted to spend the rest of my life with. When I'd circled all the wagons around my story, she said: 'I cannot begin to imagine what you have gone through, what you've seen, what you've experienced, but you don't have to go through it alone.'

Which, essentially, I had, up to that point. I'd found this person who understood, but didn't profess to know what it was like, but could empathise. I knew I wanted to be with her, intrinsically I truly believed – and why I did remains a mystery – that this woman would save me. Or certainly offer and preserve some special moments for me. My blinkers were off, and I could see a future. Of course, that gave me the wobbles, the mental sweats, the paranoia, brought on by PTSD. If thinking you've left the kettle on scares you out of your wits, imagine how this emotional turmoil plays with your brain. But Gem offered a quiet calm. Not a meek or condescending attitude but strong, caring, tough love, an instructive phrase which still doesn't really capture the total nature of what she now offers me all day, every day.

We do have some exchanges of opinions! It's mostly my fault as my PTSD puts a magnifying glass on everything.

It's often out of focus. But that's part of many people's lives – you disagree and get the hump, and then make up. My life changed for the better when I met my Gem. But deep down I knew I was walking over dangerous ground. I had my demons – should I be sharing them with someone I was beginning to care for? At many moments on many days, I'd reach a point where I didn't really care if I lived or died. Despite all the fears, I was determined to meet her, but I didn't have the balls to tell her that. Whether that was my heartfelt uncertainty about what I was embarking on or fear of rejection I'll never know.

My bloody-minded attitude kicked in. I was determined, so much so I concocted an elaborate charade to enable us to get together. It's a touch embarrassing to recall it. I was working for clients, but I'd also formed my own company offering accessibility surveys and solutions. I told Gem I had to drop some paperwork into a potential client, the Celtic Manor Hotel in Newport, near her home in Monmouthshire.

'Why don't we go there for lunch?'

That was all agreed and I whizzed over from Essex wearing a suit and tie – ready for business – and there she was looking wonderful. I sort of forgot about my excuse for being there as we talked and talked. It startled me as we came to the end of the meal – I had to do 'the work'. I'd brought my company documents, a pile of letterhead flyers, but no one in the place had a merry clue who I was. I go up to the concierge desk and ask for the general manager of the hotel and he appears, and I give him the guff: 'Following on from our conversation yesterday and the documents you requested I thought I'd just like drop them in.'

The bloke can't look at me and go 'who the bloody hell are you?' Maybe he did talk to me and being a busy man had lost that conversation. He played along with it, which was the right result, and he's going 'we've been waiting for this, thank you, fantastic'.

I do owe that man a drink for helping me out, for that was the start of my life with Gem.

It sounds so daft now, but for me at that moment it was a glimmer of a future. Gem and I had connected in person at a time when I found life itself intolerable. I know now how medically unsound I was but what's also true is that there was no safety net in or outside the system to catch me; like so many others I was the gap in the system, treated, healed, as far as possible, discharged and left to fend for myself. Gaps like me are even wider 20 years on, and that's a shaming travesty.

On the surface, and by now I was an expert in appearances, I presented as a 'cured' person but the 'triggers' which bring Khan and all the hell he carries with him back into any day of my life were full-on active. And I was suicidal.

Suicide is a selfish thing. When you get to the point where you feel like that's the only option it's fucking terrifying, as it is when you sit down and you know that you're going to end your life at that point. You get this sense of *I'm going to be free of all this* but thinking of killing yourself has its own horrors.

I felt a horror in the tunnel but the difference if you're going to do away with yourself is you say: *I'm going to control it and I'm going to do it on my terms.* I felt it was the only bit of control I had in my life, the ultimate control. I tell you this to explain my state of mind as I'm falling in love with this woman who not only understands me but is taking the time to do so. Until then people around me, I believe, saw me as an inconvenience. A shortage of time in a ferociously fast world is a useful get-out for not bothering and that makes Gem so much an exceptional saviour. But we've had our times. She fights for the last word.

That Manor Hotel lunch began my commuting life between Upminster and Wales. I won a job with a fire safety management company that wanted somebody with accessibility and construction knowledge to look at safe escape routes in an emergency evacuation. I worked out of their Manchester offices, which meant a lot of driving. I'd be there Monday, Tuesday, Wednesday night and then drive to Wales and work from Gem's for the rest of the week. On the weekend, I'd go back to Essex. I don't know how much the commuting contributed to it, but my PTSD became really, really bad. I was incredibly unwell, and I jacked the job in. I knew that I was in love with Gem, which was such a good thing for me, but the devil in the illness kept fighting me. The more I knew I wanted to be with her, the more I lost the plot, it was like living in a rather bizarre, over-the-top Hollywood-style rom-com. Or more accurately, tragicomedy.

Living for me, and with me, takes patience. Gem and I work on a ratio that if we have more good days of laughing than we do bad days of crying, we're winning.

But, and I must emphasise, it needs patience. On both sides. In those early days of knowing Gem in 2013 when I was confused and commuting, we decided to have a quiet weekend in Eastbourne when I was working down on the south coast, a little sea air for the body and the soul and the health of the relationship. It didn't go that well. Gem says it was hell on earth. I'd dithered about taking her away. I invited her, I then changed my mind before changing it again, and we had a good old row before we even left Wales. We drove down to Eastbourne pretty much in silence.

We checked into the hotel and went for a meal. Gem didn't want to eat anything. We had a shouting match instead of the meal, and she stormed off. It's about 10.30pm, and she's just fucked off. I'm following her in my wheelchair, and she walked up some concrete steps thinking I couldn't get up them. I jumped out of the chair onto my arse trying to climb these steps and crawling through glass, cutting myself. It was crazy and then we settled and found ourselves in the car park.

We sat in our car and then drove around having a heart to heart. We parked by a garage and Gem got some cigarettes and she's smoking and there's a great petroleum lorry next to us. I'm freaking, thinking we're all going to be blown up to kingdom come. But, as always, we settled. The pendulum swung, the drama of relationships, like setting the right time on your watch.

The next day was good. I'd given a talk – I can push PTSD to one side to do something, and then it rages back – and we drove over to Beachy Head. The irony of that being a favoured suicide spot isn't lost on me. Gem went for a walk, and I was watching her from the car, and remember, we hadn't known each other very long, but I absolutely adored her, I loved her to bits. I sat in the car watching this beautiful woman walking to the edge of the cliff to take some photos and I thought: *You can't do this to her, it's not fair, you must make this stop.*

I knew I couldn't simply break it off, say I don't want to see you anymore, for I knew I'd be drawn straight back to her. When we got back to Wales, one of Gem's cats was missing, but after a couple of hours we found Reggie safe and well. This was a Wednesday, and I told Gem I had to get back to Essex to do a couple of bits and I'd be back at the weekend. We could get back on track then. I gave her a kiss and a cuddle and drove off. The next day, back in Upminster, I decided she deserved better than what I could offer. I tried to hang myself.

I'd spent time looking into how to kill myself, for I didn't want it to be messy if people were coming to view my dead body in the Chapel of Rest.

It was all so crystal clear, the solution to all the heartache.

I wheeled into my bedroom and parked up by the

wardrobe where I'd decided to hang myself. I shoved some of the hanging clothes out of the way, for I wanted to get on with it. I'm a bit of a lump so I thought the weight would work for me. I leaned forward into the wardrobe, released the brakes on my wheelchair, pushed it back as I pushed forward, the idea being I'd drop and snap my neck. I dropped alright, with a right bloody bump on my arse as the fucking pole broke.

I'm sitting in the bottom of the wardrobe half laughing and half crying: *you can't even fucking kill yourself, you idiot.* I'm sitting there with all the clothes about me like someone's lost laundry thinking, Narnia isn't supposed to be like this. It's kind of funny now but then it was despair, a bitter aggravation. I'd have to do better at killing myself.

It was most premeditated, but no one would ever have known what I was about to do. Gem wouldn't have let me leave Wales if she'd had any inkling that I would try suicide. I really can present a poker face to the world.

With Gem, I went on the missing list. I didn't want to make contact, fearing I wouldn't be able to go ahead and kill myself. I went to see my GP and said I was struggling. Sleeping tablets and antidepressants were prescribed – that happens a lot, one of the many glaring examples of the misunderstanding and crass treatment of those suffering PTSD and other mental disorders – the GP had no under-standing of what he was dealing with. He also prescribed painkillers.

I went to my local Tesco, filled out the prescription and

went off for a cup of coffee while I waited for it. I picked up the pills, bought a bottle of Scotch, and went home and had a party. I laid all my medication out, all my painkillers and sedatives, and sat there chucking pills down and drinking Scotch. I did a bottle of Bells. And fucked it up again.

I was knocked out for two days. I woke up covered in my own puke and blood and God knows what else. I spent a week in bed, absolutely in bits, and damaged my liver a little as a result of what I'd done.

When I properly got it together, I was really pissed off that [A] I'd woken up and [B] I'd made a complete mess of my bed. None of that deterred me from wanting to kill myself but some instinct made me contact Gem. She was frantic, not knowing whether I was dead or alive. I put my everything-is-okay mask on, inside I was screaming, and went over to Wales.

This was November 2013, and she knew that things weren't right. She didn't know that it was as bad as me trying to end my life. I got through that trip, but I never left that bad space in my head and when I got back to the bungalow, I went for the suicide hat trick. They say trying to kill yourself is a cry for help. It's not if you reach a stage where you're prepared to sling tablets down your throat and neck off a bottle of Scotch.

You're not playing at it. If you ring people up and say you're going to do it, then that's a cry for help. I wanted to die. I got more pills, the prescription was conveniently on repeat and went to buy things to gas myself in the car.

I'd written a bunch of letters, I never thought of them as suicide notes. They said that I felt what I was doing was for the best, for everyone including myself. I collected my packs of pills, half a bottle of Scotch and quite late in the evening I drove to the local country park, part of which I knew would be open.

I parked up and went round to the back, I nearly burned myself on the exhaust pipes, a silly thing to worry about in the circumstances; I wanted it all over. I prepared the car and laid out the tablets on the dashboard alongside the letters to Gem and my mum and dad. My car had a push button start and I was just about to start the action when a park ranger saw me and came running over and started banging on the car. He'd seen the car with the engine off, but the battery was on and the brake lights were spotlighting what I was doing.

I roared up the engine and slung it in reverse and there's a big plume of smoke in a great *whoosh*. I all but ran him over as I tear-arsed in reverse. I pushed the hoses out the windows as I drove off, and as I was flying out of there, the end bits snapped out of the exhausts. He had no time to ID the car. The tablets went flying with the letters off the dashboard. Maybe there's a message there. I drove about in a daze, lost in every sense, and then I took off to Southend.

I sat in the car on the seafront and I cried, thinking: *I can't keep doing this, I've got to get help, accept help, or I've got to kill myself fucking properly. I can't keep fucking up.*

I rang Gem the next day. And I was honest.

'Look, I'm sorry, but you need to know something.'

'What is it?'

'I've tried to kill myself. I don't think I can get through this anymore.'

She didn't mess about: 'If you don't come to me tomorrow, then I will be ringing the police. I love you but you're dangerous, you can't be on your own. You're going to have to be taken care of. I can do that, or I can ring the police and have you sectioned.'

I went to bed that night but didn't really sleep and cried most of the night. I was on the phone with Gem during the night and drove off to Wales in the morning. I'd confessed my suicide attempts to Gem and mentally that made it worse, if that makes sense, because for me, it was like I've now put more pressure on her. I've made the situation even more difficult for her. And again, the vicious circle that is my PTSD mind dictates the only way I can solve this is to extricate myself from it. The urge to kill myself was still there and still is sometimes. It was a Sunday on the M4, and I was in the fast lane going along and I saw this container lorry in the slow lane in front of me. I'm blinking my eyes, and I see Khan staring at me. His eyes locked on me. I wasn't out of it because I consciously indicated across the lanes and at about 300 metres behind the lorry I thought *fuck it* and accelerated with Khan's face as the bullseye.

I use powerful cars, and the car fucking took off. I shut my eyes, and I saw Gem's face and thought *you stupid prick,* you can't do this. I braked, squealing and swerving onto the shoulder, just missing the lorry.

I got myself together and drove on to Gem and fell into her arms. I pleaded with her to help me. She did, absolutely, in every way you can imagine. She stepped up where everyone else has stepped away. And they were big steps. I'm here now, and I'm taking into account everything Adrian did in the tunnel, what the genius doctors and nurses did in the hospital, and I can truthfully say I wouldn't be if it wasn't for her. We didn't know each other that well. I loved her to bits, but we weren't in a full-blown relationship; we were – pardon the pun – still finding our feet with each other. Yet, never once did it become too much trouble. The world would understand if she'd said she couldn't cope. I put her through a living hell, disappearing and behaving as I did.

The PTSD me thought that was the sensible thing, the only way to make all this nastiness of 7/7 go away was to die. But the normal me looks back and thinks: you could have destroyed the best thing that you've ever had. I did so much damage, and I'm very lucky that Gem was able to move beyond that. From 2013 – the time we got together – if I hadn't had her in my life, I know I would have driven the car off a cliff to make sure I did kill myself, to eradicate all the trauma. My suffering finishes, I'm in the ground, leaving the trauma of me dying for everyone else.

PTSD doesn't allow you to see things logically, you get fixated on the solution. And for my fucked-up brain the solution to make things better for me was suicide. Anybody that says suicide is a selfish thing wants to hope to God that they're never in a position where they feel that that's the only option they've got. When you get to that point it is fucking terrifying. When you decide that's it, that's the only way to be free, it's frightening. You're going to die, be gone. Everything I felt in that tunnel, I was putting myself through again, the fear of dying. It's such a paradox. The difference this time was I was going to die on my terms. The only control I had in my life was ending my life. Oh, you feel like you're the boss but the reality is you live or die and without Gem dragging me through the absolute hell I was in – showing me a green light, hope of a future – I'd have been gone. So much troubled me. I'd go back to 2009 when my Nan died. I never grieved for her, I didn't have the space in my head.

When she passed away it was another thing to add to the list. At the funeral my mother is in bits, my auntie and uncle are so very upset. And I'm sitting there, completely numb to it. I'm asking myself, *why aren't you in tears?* My normal was on a different scale but I was oblivious to that. I was angry at myself for not being upset.

My depression and my PTSD are like falling into a deep, dark hole in the ground and being trapped for what seems like an eternity. The difference now is Gem jumps in with me.

The first time she hunkered down with me in the bedlam my mind can be, I'm thought: *She's as mad as I am. Why the hell would she want to do this?*

The magic is that she knows the way out. She guides my escape. The only way with PTSD is to keep pushing through it because today might be bad, tomorrow might be bad, but the next day might not. And, if it's not the next day that's good, it might be the next week or the next month or the next year. But if you keep pushing through it, with the right support, those good times will be there again.

The reason I'm being so personal, revealing all this turmoil, is because I want to elaborate for those who may be suffering – and there are countless doing so in silence – so they might understand that it doesn't matter how big you are, how tough you are, with something like this you cannot do it on your own. I'd challenge anyone to battle the demons I have and do it on their own.

The difficulty is not only wanting help but finding it.

I was reluctant, Khan was always lurking, but I was lucky.

Chapter Twelve

PSYCHODRAMA

'We loved with a love that was more than love.'
– EDGAR ALLAN POE, ANNABEL LEE, 1849

BY NOW YOU'LL HAVE got the message that there's a lot of love and pain entangled with Complex PTSD but that's also exacerbated by our day-to-day lives.

I struggle with almost every facet of living, from getting out of bed to getting a cup or a glass from a shelf in the cupboard. It sounds mundane but if you think of what you did in the past 20 minutes, be it climb the stairs or make a cup of tea or stand under the shower – the joy of that possibility – these are things I can't do or have to do very differently.

That's just an inkling of it. Gem has to watch me struggle and be pig-headed and stubborn and saying 'I can do it' and being too proud to say 'help us out here'.

Of course, sometimes I can't cope. I properly knew that when Gem persuaded me to go to Wales and, in time, to find treatment. When you go through massive trauma like I did, you feel toxic and like you can affect other people with this misery. Gem gave me hope that life was possible again.

I told her: 'I am as broken as you can get, you have your whole life ahead of you, why do you want to spend it with someone like me?'

And her response was: 'It's not who you are right now that matters, it's who you can be, and that's what we are working on.'

And we did and are. I had somebody that, if I woke up screaming, was there to comfort me and let me know that I'm safe, I'm not back in that tunnel. It's not happening all over again. It's those little things that make a world of difference when you have flashbacks –you've got somebody that will bring you out of it and let you know you're safe. Truly, in my case, a lifesaver. That was the turning point for me. I could address what happened to me, face the fact that I've got a very severe physical disability and admit I needed help and, most importantly, be thankful for it.

At that point I was in the middle of a severe mental breakdown. Khan would rampage around my head every day, climbing in the window, and about to plunge his hand into the ever-present rucksack. I still reach a point sometimes where life is actually worse than death. And that's a scary place to be. I'm living on that cliff edge every day, every week. But I cope because of the treatments which evolved from December 2013.

I'd driven from Upminster on a Sunday with many mis-givings. On the Monday morning we were in Caffe Nero for a coffee when Gem recognised I was having a nervous breakdown. She organised for me to be seen at Maindiff Court Hospital near Abergavenny, Monmouthshire, as a psychiatric patient. It was a famous place, she said. I'd be following the footsteps of Rudolf Hess, Hitler's deputy, known as the Kaiser of Abergavenny who was held there in June 1942 when it was a Prisoner of War facility. Looking back now, it wasn't that convincing an argument.

When we got there, I refused to get out of the car, being the stubborn bastard that I am, and she went in and spoke to the psychiatric nurse who persuaded me. I laid it all on the line: how I felt and what had happened with my suicide attempts.

The nurse said they could admit me – I'd be sectioned – or if Gem felt comfortable looking after me for 24 hours, I could be assessed the following day, and that's what happened.

I had to get through Christmas and into the New Year and, with difficulty, I did. Maindiff Court referred me to psychiatrist Bob Colter who, for me, was a visionary. As ever, I was reluctant to put myself in the hands of others. Especially on 14 January 2014 when I first saw where he worked.

St Cadoc's Hospital at Caerleon near Newport is one of those old country lunatic asylums of the 1880s, all Vincent Price and *The Fall of the House of Usher*. Hammer Horror without the cleavage or the cobwebs. I drove by the gates and down this long, sweeping driveway to this fucking terrifying looking building with gargoyles above the door. There's a building next to it that's got this green cage over the garden so people can't escape. I looked at Gem and I'm thinking: *You can get fucked if you think I'm going in there, there's no way.* She's reading my mind.

'No, come on. We need to do this or that's it.'

Eventually, she persuaded me into the consulting room with Bob Colter, who'd then been a Clinical Psychologist for more than 25 years. What Gem discovered was he'd also been Clinical Director in the NHS Mental Health Service in Gwent, Wales, and ran a specialist psychological service for people with extreme difficulties in managing their emotional states – helping people like me.

On offer was a choice of Cognitive Behaviour Therapy, Dialectical Behaviour Therapy, Mentalisation Based Therapy, Cognitive Analytic Therapy, Eye Movement Desensitisation and Reprocessing, Mindfulness and Acceptance and Commitment Therapy. All a mystery to me but Bob Colter simplified it: 'Tell me your story.'

I was hesitant.

He quizzed me: 'What is stopping you? Why do you not want to do this? '

I stuttered out: 'For me this is Pandora's box. I'm terrified that once I take the fucking lid off, I'm never going to get it back on.'

He looked at me, shook his head, sat back, crossed his

legs, and grinned: 'What makes you think this has ever had a lid on it? You're not opening this up, you're living it right now. It can't get any worse than this, it can only get better. There ain't been a lid on this box for years. You're about as traumatised as you can get.'

He explained I needed special therapy but he could help me. And he was very clear. He said: 'Look, PTSD isn't something you can be cured of, but I can teach you the coping mechanisms.'

I really respected that because he was brutally honest with me. He was going to use EDMR, which stands for Eye Movement Desensitisation and Reprocessing with the information bumf being:

> *This is a powerful and effective method for address-ing and resolving psychological trauma that is causing ongoing distress. It uses eye movements whilst thinking about the past traumas experienced which enables your natural automatic adaptive corrective processing to become freed up so that this psychological adjustment can happen and resolve the trauma.* [www.emdrasso-ciation.org.uk]

At first, he didn't focus on the trauma itself but on my state of mind, inner feelings and anxieties, all of it, the self-hatred and survivor guilt. It began. I sat in front of Bob, and he waved his hand and asked me to follow it with my eyes and talk. Now, I'm a down-to-earth Essex boy and I'm thinking: *This is a load of bullshit. It's bollocks, Some soppy twat waving at me like he's directing traffic ain't gonna do fuck all. Feel free to fuck right off. Immediately*

But I sat there. He's waving and saying, all but chanting, 'follow my hand', and my brain started throwing up all of these memories and everything was unreal. In time he took me back to the tunnel, but from a different perspective – until this EMDR I'd always been in the middle of the action, blaming myself for so much including cowardice and inaction. The EMDR therapy took me back there but from a spectator's point of view.

I saw myself objectively for the first time and my warped brain began to understand that I never had any way of stopping the devastation caused by Khan and his gang, neither physically nor emotionally. I didn't force Khan to set off the bomb. I couldn't help the others. I know this makes such obvious sense but to me it never did. I was in intensive treatment having one-hour sessions four times a week. I was being rewired. I'm making it sound straightforward but, believe me, the wires so very often got tangled.

I do so much want to explain myself for I'd been in the Twilight Zone up to working with Bob Colter. I've got Complex PTSD, and how that differs from PTSD is somebody with PTSD will have a trigger, and they'll remember their trauma. Somebody with Complex PTSD, it's almost as if part of my brain is still in that tunnel.

When I'm triggered, it's not that I remember my trauma, I relive it. With Complex PTSD, I suffer from depression, I've got obsessive compulsive disorder (OCD), and I suffer from anxiety. So these are all the things that kind of get wrapped up in a nice ball and dumped on you.

I can safely say, if it wasn't for Gem and Bob, I wouldn't be here today. I believe there was only two or three months left before I successfully killed myself. Everything was pointing that way. My only choice was to be locked away forever, a mental case, or learn to live like other people. And learn to be me again, the old me – not physically, that can never be – but to be myself in my head.

My treatment went on for many weeks and I'd be so tired and try not to go in, but Gem dragged me there whether I was kicking or screaming or not. Then, after the session, she'd be there, and the world would be right again. Every time I didn't think I could do it, but I did because of Gem. The great leap for me was, as I explained, the EMDR therapy directing my mind to see it from the view of an outside observer, where I was a victim and not a perpetrator of the suffering in any way and, crucially, not at fault. I was not to blame for anything. I couldn't have prevented the disaster or stopped people dying. Nevertheless, subliminally, I needed something I thought unobtainable – proof.

Yes, my mind is a crazy whirl. Remember, I must check if I've left the kettle plugged in. How do I check I've got my mind straight about the tunnel? I talked to Gem about it and we decided I had to confront my demons. I had to return to Edgware Road.

I shiver to think of it. Gem arranged it with the people at Edgware Road Tube station. On 18 July 2014 we arrive outside the place, park up in the disabled bay, and I wheel my chair into the open and there's the blue and white Tube sign and I think: *That's advertising 7/7.* I was outside for about an hour, terrified that I couldn't confront this. Eventually, Gem made the decision for me and found the station manager. She took over my wheelchair and told me we were going in.

There were a load of the train station staff waiting for me – some of them remembered seeing me being carried out. I'm frozen to the spot; my mind feels like it's filled with cement. Two of the Tube guys, Steve and Alex, are right down-to-earth blokes who were there on 7/7. Steve tells me they all thought I was dead, *everyone* thought I was a *goner.* Alex asked me if I fancied going down onto the platform to see the tunnel. My heart's doing panic somersaults, and I feel I'm suffocating. I all but scream *No!* in panic. I asked Gem to go down to the platform and take some photos, to which she replied: 'No.'

She was concerned and told me: 'If you are going to do this, do it properly.' She's holding my hand and saying she'd be with me all the time and I need to beat the fear. This is a to-hell-and-will-I-get-back moment. Where I got the strength of purpose, I don't know but I go for it. Of course, the absurdity of it, is my wheelchair is too big to negotiate the not-at-all disability friendly station.

The Tube guys grab a lighter wheelchair they keep at the station, and I climb on board, and they manoeuvre me about as they carry me down the stairs to the platform –

into the exact same position I was in when I was stretchered out in bits and pieces the day of the bomb. I'm staring
at that fucking ceiling and I'm hearing that tumult of
voices, the screams, the terror. Gem squeezes my hand
as the guys guide me down on to the platform with
commuters wondering why this bloke's getting the red-
carpet treatment. The tunnel shakes with a train approaching. I'm determined not to cry, but it's tough. The PTSD
brain is in direct conflict with the EMDR-tutored one. I
was in what was the depths of hell for me on that Tube
platform, and with every train that passed I was ready for
an explosion. Did I want to get on a train? Did I fuck. But
I might…

Trains whizzed back and forward and finally I got up the
nerve and we boarded one, the same second carriage as 7/7.
I showed Gem where Khan sat and how close I was to him.
She could see how distraught I was, I was sweating and
shivering; Gem had tears running down her face. The train
went through a tunnel, it went all dark, and that's when I
got really scared. And then suddenly, the train came to a
sudden stop in the tunnel, and I thought that I was about
to freak out. The station manager, who was with us, calmed
my thoughts. He turned to me and said: 'Tell me what was
the first thing you saw, the first thing you remembered.'

I said, I remembered the number '4' painted white on the
tunnel wall and I didn't know why. He looked at me and
pointed at the number '4' on the wall – he had told the train
driver to stop the train exactly where the bomb had gone

off. I'm looking outside the train at the spot where I thought I'd end my days. I feel sick, Gem has her arms around me, but I'm feeling comforted by being there, facing my devil in his den. I'm thinking: *I'm not there, Khan is, bits of the real him, not the phantom tormentor, are still there stuck in this underworld with the vermin... we probably just rolled over some of him... but I'm going out into the sunlight.*

I ordered Khan to stay put but I knew his ghost wouldn't, that insidious little bastard spectre will never get that message. It was a packed train, and the passengers had been told who I was and they, with great consideration, sat there in silence, like a minute of silence, for the tragedy of it all. Gem and I were in a right state. The train pulled away, heading to the next stop, Paddington, where I should've got off on 7/7.

As the train moved, I felt this lead weight being lifted from my shoulders and from my soul. I was going to finish that train journey, and I was going to get off that train with the woman I absolutely adored and head into the beautiful sunshine in London. I wanted to live the life I live now and not be shackled by the past. I'm a firm believer in hope. I think even if the world goes to absolute shit around you, if you've got hope, something to cling to and something to fight for, it can get better.

I knew I'd changed following EMDR. Previously, I just felt toxic. I felt that 7/7 had put a level of toxicity into me that I could then transfer onto other people. My mindset had swerved and I realised fully that suicide is a final symptom of mental illness, and people don't understand that. They don't understand how you feel at that point when you know that within the next hour, you're not going to exist anymore, your life is going to be over. And for me, there was the sadness of not being able to explore what me and Gem could have been, but there was a relief that the suffering stops for everybody, almost like taking me out of the equation, the suffering stops for everybody, because that's what you believe.

The brain, when you're in that kind of crisis moment, is warped. Solutions you conjure up are demented. One of the big things for me was that after the explosion, being blown out of the train and witnessing everything, I couldn't do anything to help anybody. I suffer from survivor's guilt, but when I was trying to kill myself, it was within my control to protect others, and I clung to that. *I can stop the pain, I can regain control, and I can make the world a better place.* It was only when I started the treatment, and things developed with Gem, that – and, I suppose, it was sanity returning – I realised I would have harmed her and that would be the most heartbreaking thing for me.

Most importantly, I would have missed out on the amazing life that I've now got. Is it fate? What is it? I'd love someone to explain but it's wonderful how horrible things can turn out to be positive. It's quite astonishing.

Yeah, yeah, I know you'll think I'm still not all there, but I feel that. In that moment in time when I was really, mentally unwell, death seemed like the perfect solution.

The opposite was true. I didn't need to protect people, I needed to embrace them, and their help and support and love.

I should have been charging full steam towards it because that's when you get better. You have to ask to be better. Gem was prepared to sacrifice so much for me, and I wanted a future with her, but I was terrified that I'd destroy her. I needed to protect her from me, not because I was violent or any nonsense like that, but just because I was so broken that I didn't think I could ever be put back together in any shape. It was that process of pushing through that enabled me to get the treatment and get to where we are today.

Which is surviving. On the precipice.

Every day I'm never more than 30 seconds away from my next PTSD episode.

It really is exhausting but looking at life now and thinking back to my apprehension as I approached St Cadoc's Hospital, I could have never in a million years imagined I would be as up for our daily fight with life.

It is a battle. We go out and laugh and joke and hold hands in the car and we can be having a normal day and then the PTSD will hit, but now I've learned to cling onto that little bit of a normal day. These little snippets of light are great, but Gem is like a fucking great beacon in my life, and I work through second by ticking second.

The wonderful miracle is believing in myself. The day-to-day pressures of disability – and the spectre of Khan – didn't vanish and there were other obstacles to overcome.

Especially when I left the relative safety of the Upminster bungalow and set up home with Gem in September 2014. It wasn't simply moving house; it was going from a home designed for my needs to one that wasn't disability friendly.

Being together gave us enormous strength to deal with everything including, literally, shit. To rephrase Mariah Carey: All I wanted for Christmas was a commode.

Chapter Thirteen

LOVE IS

'It's only a paper moon.'
– HAROLD ARLEN, E.Y. HARBURG, BILLY ROSE,
THE GREAT MAGOO, 1933

IT WAS A MOST sensational day for me when I moved permanently to Wales, yet it was a little crowded as Khan, of course, moved in too. Happily, I was learning more and more how to cope with his appearances rather than diving under the duvet.

Dealing with bureaucracy was sometimes as challenging. You'd think I'd tick the boxes as someone needing occasional help, but we had to bang on doors to get what little we requested. We never asked for anything that wasn't needed, we were not chasing after a plasma TV or a Jacuzzi. Just somewhere to go to the toilet.

Gem's place had an upstairs bedroom and bathroom which was inaccessible for me. From day one I had to leave the house and go to the toilet in town – if it wasn't closed

– or wait till the local Waitrose opened at 8am. When we were waiting to get a bed sorted at the living level, Gem's neighbours invited us to sleep over there. Again, the toilet was upstairs so when I needed to go in the middle of the night, I found myself very quietly trying to get out of the house down a metal ramp – and that made a noise like the end of the world – to get in the car to drive to town and use a public toilet. I'm wide awake and stay that way through the night, and Gem is too. She's watching me, it's early days, because of fears of a PTSD attack.

Coming up to Christmas was a problem – the shops which offered me access to disabled toilets were going to be shut. We contacted Adult Social Services explaining this and asked for a commode. They wouldn't help and there didn't seem to be any rhyme nor reason to their refusal. Obstinance for obstinance's sake is what it felt like it. They suggested I could go into a nursing home – and Gem could live there too! Hey ho. They relented, after Gem gave them a badgering, and tried to locate a commode – apparently, it's easier to find *Doctor Who* in Wales. When they did, the social services wouldn't drop it off, so we had to arrange for it to be collected and delivered. And there the commode stood in our kitchen – for two years.

In the Hollywood movies there's the cool images of the married couple with one in the bath and the other sitting on the toilet. Our reality was somewhat different as my kitchen became my bathroom.

It sounds disgusting but it became our norm, it was all

we had. Disposal of such waste then becomes the issue to overcome and you have to be quite creative to do so. With the bathroom inaccessible, I had to have bed baths and that ruined a few mattresses.

I look back on it now and think not many people have lived what we've lived through to be happy and for two people that love each other to be together. Gem also chose me over a certain family member, for they told her she'd spend her life as a carer, that I was a burden and I wouldn't be good enough. Gem saw the person as in their own bubble and left them to it, but I do feel sad about that.

It seems we need to compromise all the time with human relations. If I get on with someone, I'm a friend for life, but if someone doesn't care for me that's fine too, not a problem for me. What is galling is when people make judgments and don't know what I am capable of, don't take the time to consider what disabled people can do and can contribute.

On one shopping trip, when Gem was poorly, I had a close encounter of the unpleasant kind. There are two types of supermarket trollies that go on a wheelchair. One has little claws that clip on both sides and another with two clamps that you have to tighten up but as you're tightening one up, the other one drops. Trying to do them together isn't easy, especially without legs. My luck, that's the only one available, my back's killing me as I'm leaning forward and fiddling about, and it took me a good 20 minutes of messing around to get this bloody thing clipped to the front of me. I'm in a flap. I want to get us something for dinner that's quick and easy to prepare and I pick one of those pizzas stacked with UFOs, unidentified frying objects.

A guy comes up to me: 'That's a lovely meal for someone like you living on their own.'

Now, I'm not in that cheerful a mood with all the faffing about. But I say: 'I'm sure my wife will really appreciate it.'

The frozen meals section man stutters: 'You're married? I didn't think somebody like you would be married.'

If I hadn't been sitting down I would have had to. It's condescending, callous and cruel because he didn't, and people don't, think of the effect of being stupid. I also get the downright nasties. I've been to Tesco and there was a geezer standing in the fridge section. And what I wanted to get was in front of him. I said 'excuse me' three times and he ignored me. Made it clear he was doing that on purpose.

'I've asked you three times politely, now I'm telling you to move.'

He leans down into me, his face in my face, and he curses and tells me: 'People like you shouldn't even be allowed out on your own.'

He walked off, trailing his ignorance. People will never fail to surprise me and that day I thought it would be worth three months inside – I'd be in the medical wing – to have given him a belt. It's part of disabled life, being a nuisance to some.

On another Tesco trip, this bloke was standing in front of the shelf and I wheeled up next to him and waited patiently for him to move over, giving him his own time, to allow me to get to the milk cartons. He didn't budge.

'Excuse me, mate.'

He turns and looks at me as if I'm an unflushed lavatory. He snarled: 'What you doing here, getting in people's way?'

I couldn't be arsed to make something of it. Didn't need the stress.

If people like me and accept me for who I am– and I'm foul-mouthed company, a building site boy – that's wonderful, but I don't go out of my way to be friends with people. I am polite and always aware I'm taking up space with my wheelchair and accommodate for that. I don't want to be treated differently, for that exacerbates the disability. I don't have a particularly big circle of friends. I don't crave people liking me.

What annoyed me most about the breakdown between Gem and her relative was them implying she was stupid to be with somebody who's going to be a burden. Which, yes, I am, in my mind, but she always tells me I'm not. We were a couple dealing with it. She is on my side and thank the Lord for that. And, of course, none of them knew the half of living with someone like me. I don't give a toss what people say about me. But insulting Gem is like a red rag to a bull. When I first moved in, everything was a panic for me and very much for her. What to expect?

People misunderstand what Post Traumatic Stress Disorder is. It doesn't give me the sniffles or a cough or anything like that. What it does, when it's bad, is sap the life out of you. You feel physically drained with absolutely no energy. On awful days, I wouldn't shave or shower. Her house being inaccessible, we slept on the sofa, and I'd be awake most of the night watching telly. She'd wake up tired and get herself ready for work. She'd come home and I'd be in exactly the same position. With the cat asleep beside me. I never made food or got a drink and stared at endless episodes of telly nonsense. Gem was learning to work with me but, cleverly, she didn't trust me. She always made sure if she had to work I was never alone, that someone was there to babysit me to ensure I didn't do anything stupid.

When I look back on it, I can't understand how she focused at work when she didn't know if she's going to walk in and find me dead on the floor having cut my wrists, taken a massive overdose or packed up and gone and ploughed my car into a wall. She had no way of knowing until she came through the door.

The bombings, any atrocity, had a knock-on effect on those close to the victims, whether those victims were killed or maimed. It hurt Gem by proxy, being the person I'm closest to. In the aftermath, almost everything I went through, she went through as well, just without the visuals of it, because I'm the one seeing Khan come for tea or climb in the window when the PTSD announces his entrance.

She so wanted to understand what I'd gone through in the tunnel, to identify the black hole where I lay, that one day when I had a meeting in London, she left me at my appointment and went to Edgware Road. She got some idea of the darkness and the despair but there was not the noise, the frightened, frantic mayhem, the hellish chorus being played at full volume which is a constant in my head.

We understand each other but explaining can't replace experiencing it. A 2008 telly documentary on Channel 4 called *The Angels of Edgware Road* helped her understand when we cranked it up on YouTube. And it shocked me.

There were a lot of heroes on 7/7, and Adrian and I decided not to participate in the film, so I hadn't a clue what was in it. There was a bit of footage used in the programme I'd never seen. As the bomb goes off on the train I'm on there's a train coming up the other way and both are stuck in the tunnel, side by side after the blast. As people are getting out of the train, some have climbed across into the bombed carriage to try and help, and others are making their way out the tunnel. A guy in the second train has filmed on his mobile phone and you hear me screaming for help.

It's blood curdling, with me begging for somebody to come and find me. When I heard the scream, I knew it was me. I remember what I was shouting: *Help me, somebody please help me, for God's sake, somebody help me.* When I think of it at this moment, I can hear it, the anguish of it locked in my head. My screams are like the throes of somebody dying and begging for any God to come and find them and save them. It was no time to be agnostic.

When Gem heard me screaming my lungs out, in that context, with the emergency lighting casting dark shadows, and the noise, that was a touch of the evil from that day. The ten seconds I'm screaming my head off is me in a panic and certain I'm going to die, thinking I'm within 20 seconds of being dead. When you hear it for real there's nothing that compares to the absolute abject terror, because I'm fucking terrified. It was quite surreal to sit there with Gem watching it and then sit bolt upright knowing it was me – the accent, the fucking swearing – for it's quite something to hear. You'd never think you'd hear yourself dying. And I was on the way to the grave until help arrived.

Life has been turbulent since the attack, but 20 or more years on, I've learned to glide over most of the bumps. There are horrendous days magnified by my PTSD mind but getting on and making a living is a fight for most people. In the first years making home with Gem, I was desperate to prove my worth and work would be going well only to be bulldozed from me by PTSD attacks when I didn't have the energy to fulfil my roles. In time, I became my own boss but all the time the mission was to pay my way and help promote better access for the disabled, in everything from Premier League football stadiums to the loo around the corner on any high street, to your own home.

In Wales, I had another go at walking. I went back as an outpatient but, as I explained, because of the nature of my injuries it makes it a million times harder to try and use the prosthetics. Yet, there's always this niggling part of you that goes, *well, just give it one more try.* I'm a little embarrassed because when you read this you're going to be thinking: *If you can walk, why don't you use the legs?*

The public perception is one of the great frustrations an amputee like me has.

On TV when you see military personnel with lost limbs, they're in hospital with stumps in bandages, and the next clip is them walking across a parade ground to get a medal. The bit they don't show is the ball-breaking effort it takes to do that. So many people have this assumption, *oh, you lose your legs, it's fine, they give you a metal set, and off you go.*

The reality is totally different to that. It breaks you physically and emotionally. What I suffered most again was the emotional side – when I stood up, it felt amazing. Walking was painful, which is emphasised by the statistics: if you're a double above knee amputee, it takes 800 percent more energy to take one step than it does for somebody with their own legs. Imagine the amount of energy that takes when I've got respiratory issues from the blast, and I'm deaf in one ear and blind on one side, so everything goes against me for balance.

I told you how pig-headed I was about using prosthetics at Roehampton, a true pain in the arse, and I really pushed to be able to walk because the hospital said I couldn't.

I was like, 'fuck that – you're not going to decide that for me, I'll decide that for myself'. I always try to get people to understand that my physicality as a disabled man is nothing compared to my determination and drive to be successful, to live my life to the fullest I can. I believe you can overcome a lot of things with drive and determination

– *I'm not going to give up, and I will find a way* – and that's how I've had to live my life.

The legs were, and it's my old joke, one step too far. When I stood up, my phantom limb pain went immediately because my brain said that's how I should be, upright. The problem was as ever, that I had to take the fake legs off at some point and go through that emotional trauma of losing my legs. Every time. I don't ever like to be defeatist, but it became too much.

When I was in hospital I had no concept of prosthetic legs. I imagined that I'd get fitted with these super bionic legs, and life would go back to normal, better than normal for I'd be running around like Lee Majors in *The Six Million Dollar Man*. Everything would be hunky dory. Well, what did I know? The legs weren't for me. It was just too painful to have the memories of playing football and playing squash and boxing and putting these things on with a pair of joggers and a pair of trainers, knowing I could never do the things I did before. That's the thing –it's the memory again. It's the brain telling you that last week you could but today you can't. With my severe amputations, the tin legs were never going to work for me, but I didn't want to give up, I wanted to get back what I'd lost.

What makes sense to me, and I hope to you, is the prosthetic legs were a reminder of what I lost without giving me back anything of what I lost.

That's recurring pain. Part of my brain, and a part of me, is still living on the floor of that tunnel, and it will forever.

People say to me, professionals included, about suffering with trauma that my fears may not manifest, arguing 'it might never happen'. I'm not worried about what might happen. I'm terrified by what's already happened. Haunted by it. That's why it's *Post* Traumatic Stress Disorder. The memory of being blown up is installed inside me. I can't look away. It's inside me, like a poison, and on the worst of days it is suffocating and oppressive.

I'll offer a perspective as I know it's difficult if your mind is not, like mine, a jigsaw with a missing piece. In Roehampton I spoke with someone who'd lost his legs through diabetes, – this sounds really crass, and I don't mean it to be – but that was all he lost. As horrendous as that was, there were no other marks on him. Every part of my body is scarred, big scars, surgical scars; I can't even lay in bed without being reminded of what Khan did to me. I've got chunks out of my arm; I'm covered in burns. I've got physical reminders that I cannot escape. And mental ones.

When we got into a coffee shop in the reflection of the window, I'll see Khan on the other side of the road holding a rucksack. I'll be driving and I look in my rear-view mirror and he's sitting on the back seat. Or wake up and he's at the window. Now we've got the double doors, he's standing on the balcony. I will forever be linked to this dead man. He even warps my dreams for the brutal thing is, as I explained, I still dream able-bodied.

A false flag, a malicious misunderstanding, for when

I wake up every morning the first thing I look at is my wheelchair. I worked in construction, I did physical things every day that I can no longer do, and I'll never be able to do. In Wales, I had to finally acknowledge that to the day I die I'm going to be a wheelchair user – that's it. There's no going back to it, no revisiting it, because with the nature of my injuries it's a miracle that I walked on the prosthetics anyway. I had my *Rocky* moment.... and I have other moments. And they can be quite joyful. In their way.

One morning Gem and I were having breakfast in the cafe at our local Morrisons, and I lifted my glasses to rub an itch around my left eye, rather where my left eye is replaced by a prosthetic. As I'm rubbing, the 'eye' pops out onto my cheek, drops and hits the table, bounces and flips and lands in Gem's plate of baked beans. It's colour side up so staring back at me. Also staring is the woman at the next booth who I saw taking a sip of her tea as my 'eye' did acrobatics. She's spluttering at her friend who has her back to me. She bangs the table, and her friend looks around and all but freaks seeing me looking at her with a big hole in my face.

She quickly turned about as I picked the prosthetic from the beans and took it off to the bathroom to wash and put back in. The two women watched my every move.

I did a stage whisper: *I'll be back.*

And when I returned the two women were as fascinated with me as if I was Arnold Schwarzenegger. I'm used to being looked at, and I understand that I am different. But not that different. There are millions of disabled people

– the majority suffering from accidents or incidents or medical problems *after* birth.

My point is that anyone can become 'different' in a moment. Before the bombing, disability had never come into my world in any shape or form. I didn't know anybody that had a disability, it hadn't been anything that I had thought of. I'd see some people in wheelchairs and think 'that must be tough' and I'd carry on with my day with no further thought. After 7/7, I realised what can be insurmountable barriers in terms of work, education and some people seeing those with disabilities as nothing more than targets, as people that can be easily manipulated, coerced or abused and hurt.

I started to look into it further and learned about shocking accounts of disability hate crimes. The way criminal justice is stacked against a victim of a disability hate crime and if you are a witness and how much credibility you get. I looked at every facet of the life I used to live as a 26-year-old man, and then looked at the life I have now. I saw there were a lot of massive voids, pitfalls, lack of understanding and willingness to engage with those with disabilities.

I had this massive opportunity in life, having survived what no one thought I would, to make this count. I knew I might not make a huge difference in the short term but in the long run, if I keep chipping away, I hope I can make changes in the life of the next Daniel Biddle, or the next person that suffers a horrendous injury in work or in a car accident or is born with a disability.

I am lucky to be alive and feel I must do the best I can

in honour of the people who died that day. I couldn't look their families in the eye if I wasted the opportunity I've got to speak up and work for and with disabled people. If I just sat back and did nothing, then I don't think I have a right to have survived it. I want the families of people that were killed to see that I am trying to do something and I'm not wasting the opportunity I've been given.

I don't know if that will be comforting to them or not but that's the driving force that I use. I'm very lucky to have that opportunity and I certainly don't want to waste it. I want to try and make a difference, and I've got the memories from that day, of the people who died and their families, that I want to do something positive for. What gave me the stability to focus on that was Gem.

And I did something positive for myself too – we were married on 6 June 2015 in a blaze of very sweet words and smiles and wedding cake and kindly guests over-serving me beer and malt whisky. I won't make the bad joke.

My excuse for my indulgence was nerves. I know, after all the trauma, wedding day nerves! But that was the way it was. Somewhere I felt I didn't deserve to be this happy. I was expecting the bubble to burst. And Gem and her dad played with my brain by being 45 minutes late. Gem had nerves too and I love her all the more for that – she overcame them to be my wife.

Chapter Fourteen

ANGER MANAGEMENT

'There is a crack in everything, that's how the light gets in.'
–LEONARD COHEN, ANTHEM, 1992

OFFICIALLY BEING A COUPLE brought no dramatic change in our day to day lives, but it did display for me our devotion to each other. The day-to-day pressures of disability – and the spectre of Khan – did not simply disappear. They remained constant but with the PTSD under better control it meant, in turn, I could deal with the regular aggravations of living with a cleaner and more peaceful mind.

Of course, as per, I was fucking furious most days.

Channelling that anger has become a skill.

Every attempt to help the disabled, to make life that little easier is an obstacle race. You have to duck and dive and swerve around the obstinacy, the disdain, and the red tape of officialdom, having beaten the system to get through the door in the first place. I understand if someone is physically and mentally too harmed to work or want to work but millions have skills and knowledge they want to use but are prevented by circumstances or an employer not thinking outside the box.

I now run The National Diversity Employment and Advisory Services [NDEAS] to provide equity of opportunity to people with disabilities. The idea is that I find out what someone is capable of – and it might be as simple as what time of day they can work if medication makes them slow in the mornings – and dovetail them with a suitable employer, an enlightened employer who is willing to bend the workday parameters. It offers them a wider and diverse talent pool. It doesn't sound like such a sophisticated set-up, but it's been a work-in-progress for more than a decade because the biggest challenge has been educating Government and businesses about the benefits. I've met every Government Minister for Disability in the past 20 years and nothing, other than photo opportunities for them, has brought positive results. Some of them were nice enough but, ultimately, useless. I had a long conversation with David Cameron when he was Prime Minister. Pleasant enough. Same result. Sweet FA.

They all talk a good story. Stiff upper lip and carry on. It isn't alright for politicians to drive around in their bulletproof and armour-plated cars and the rest of us to suffer the consequences of their decisions. Tony Blair in particular has a large responsibility for what's happened over the past twenty years. It's innocent people that get caught up in these events and we're just expected to pay the price and crack on the best we can. Blair's a prime source of the anger which transforms into my energy.

The frustration is with the system: when it comes to disabled people and employment, we keep doing the same thing and wondering why we don't see any positive results.

The turnover in politicians responsible for the disabled is disgraceful. That role, a minister without portfolio, reporting to the Secretary of State for the Department of Work and Pensions (DWP), is not a Cabinet job but puts the holder on a career trajectory. There's a scramble to move on to a Cabinet post, meaning no one is ever in the job long enough to achieve anything. It's all self-advantage. The general attitude, I find, dismissive.

Rishi Sunak when he was a fading away Prime Minister had a go at sick-note culture, which I felt was aimed at those claiming disability benefits. Don't get me wrong, there are plenty of people out there that are playing the system for everything they can.

The problem is he tarred an entire community of people with the same brush. We need a system where as much effort goes into saying to employers, you are not inclusive enough. I met with Iain Duncan Smith when he was Secretary of State for the DWP, and I genuinely thought he had good intentions. Then he was gone, disillusioned, and replaced by Stephen Crabb, who left after claims he sent 'suggestive texts' to a 19-year-old girl.

Way before then, when Maria Miller had the disability brief, I met her at Westminster Hall in London in 2010.

Here's the usual words strung together which she said for the media/photo opportunity: 'It was fascinating to hear about Dan's experiences and his enthusiasm is inspiring. We need to get more disabled people into mainstream jobs so they can do the same work as everyone and in every sector, from hairdressing to engineering and at every level.'

It was more pissing in the wind.

I spoke at a Conservative Party Conference about creating work opportunities and better conditions for the disabled, but nothing came of that. The attitude has, ironically, been constantly sclerotic. It's almost as if they go: *That's a really good idea but if we do that, everybody's going to ask why the fuck didn't you do that 20 years ago?*

I'm not offering revolutionary ideas, but successive administrations appear to have huge embarrassment over screwing up for so long. If you fix the problem, you admit there was a problem you avoided. Take the organisation Remploy,[6] which until recent times had factories across the UK 'employing' disabled people and running, I believe, at a loss of millions of pounds a year.

They made musical instruments for schools but when the Chinese offered to make them for a fraction of the cost the contracts went to China. What happened was at the Remploy factories disabled people were being paid a wage

---

6   Remploy was established in 1949 to provide employment opportunities to disabled people. In 2015, Remploy partnered with Maximus and the Remploy brand was retired in England and Wales in 2022. It is only used in Scotland to deliver the Fair Start Scotland contract in Tayside and Lanarkshire.

but there was no work, no contracts, and it was like a social club. When the decision was made to close it, and there was much prime real estate involved, the idea was to shut the factories, sell off the land, and the factory units take that money, and reinvest it into Remploy.

Remploy would no longer receive Government subsidy but was told to go out into the commercial world and get people meaningful employment. The factories shut down, the exchequer took the money, and Remploy told the Government: 'We don't know what to do without you.' And they didn't, and they just kind of crumbled.

Subsequently, I encountered a former executive from Remploy when I took part in a Welsh Government inclusion committee, and he was boasting about the number of disabled people he got into work. But he didn't like my questions. What's the retention rate? How many are still in work after six months? He would not discuss that because the same people circulate through the machine. If they're in work for six months and they're out of work for two years, what's the point? You must have retention as part of that process.

What we do – more accurately *try* to do every day – is not only help somebody get into work but support them on their employment journey.

If, say, they're constantly late for work, we ask their line manager not to reprimand them and kick them into touch but to contact us and let us work out what's going on and devise a solution. If somebody's had a medication change and they wake up at seven o'clock in the morning like a zombie, we can change the working time if it's practical to do it. It's convincing employers and companies to think differently, otherwise it is just a revolving door: You go for an interview, get a job, you last six months. There's no support. Nobody understands. You get kicked out. You go again. Let's keep going round and round and round. That damages somebody's mental health. It damages their self-esteem to the point that they say *'fuck it'*. You can only have the door shut in your face so many times before you don't knock again. And that's what I did.

I started my own business to try to change it, and not everybody can do that. The biggest issue I have is, because the work that I do is so niche, and disability isn't looked at the way that race or religion are viewed, it always takes a backseat compared to protected characteristics.

My recruitment consultancy has a unique online jobs board, but I can't get people to buy into it because they're frightened of employing somebody with a disability. It's ridiculous. And that's where we are now, well into the 21st Century, with my own lived experience of the lack of under-standing, the inherent fear, and that whole list of myths and misconceptions I've witnessed over the years. I don't know where they started from, but they've just become fact and all the evidence that dispels them doesn't get looked at.

Box-ticking is such a threat to all of us. And a cruel aspect of employing the disabled with nonsense repeated like, 'it's a health and safety risk to employ you' or 'more expensive' as 'disabled people have more time off sick'. Why does me not having legs mean I'm going to be more prone to getting flu than you? Where's your argument? People struggle to differentiate between somebody that's disabled and somebody that's ill. I don't have an illness, I have a disability, so I'm no more likely to catch the flu than anyone else.

The other line I get is 'we can't sack a disabled person if they're no good'. And again, my argument is, well, if you're sacking me because I don't have any legs, then, no, that's discrimination. But if I'm a salesman and my job is to bring in a million pounds worth of revenue a year selling our product and after 12 months, I haven't sold a bean, that's got nothing to do with me being disabled. That's because I'm a shit salesman. If the employers say you've got two months, we'll do everything we can to support you, but after that if you're still not cutting it, you're gone – that's performance related, not disability related. People just don't understand it, and we live in a world, particularly with disability, where ignorance is almost a defence.

This is how the legislation works: the Equality Act dictates that if I apply for a job, I don't legally have to disclose the fact that I'm disabled. That's brilliant, if you've got a hidden disability, say autism or ADHD, or if you wear a hearing aid or you're slightly vision impaired; you don't need disclosure, because to look at you, nobody will know.

When I go for a position, I can see the job description, I can see the location, I can see the working hours and the salary. But I need more information, because being in the wheelchair, if I don't disclose I'm disabled, I could turn up and it could be steps into the building and I can't get to the interview.

Now, Catch-22 and three quarters. If I do disclose I'm disabled, I'm never going to get a look in. Believe me, I've tested it. I have my Daniel Biddle CV which discloses my disability, and I've got a Mick Jones CV with a Mick Jones @ Gmail email, which is completely fake, but it's the same CV, other than the name and the email address. With equal qualifications we both applied for the same job: disabled Daniel, a no, Mick Jones, asked for interview ASAP. I've done it four times with the same result.

In the early days, before Gem, when I truly needed a job for my sanity, this happened with a big supermarket chain, and I confronted them, asking if they realised it was discrimination. It freaked them and they offered all sorts, but it was a tainted brand for me.

Jobs for the disabled seems so sensible to me for it's a two-way street – an employer gets a skilled employee who clearly wants to work or for sure wouldn't be arsed to be there as the system is so askew it can be so much more financially beneficial to not bother. The mantra from politically correct officialdom is equality, equality, equality... and that's the ongoing conundrum.

Equality means treating everybody the same, right? Yet, if I'm competing with an able-bodied person for a role and the final part of the interview is whoever walks to the top of the stairs gets the job, that poses a problem. Yes, it's equal because we've both got to do the same thing. But it's not fair. There's an example given of a monkey and a goldfish at a job interview, and the interviewer says: for the sake of equality, you've both got to climb the tree. Equality is where you want to end up, but equity is what gets you there. For me, it's not a capability issue, it's an opportunity issue.

What astonishes many people is that 86% of working age disabled people in the UK acquired their disability during their 'working life'. They were not born with it but were afflicted, by whatever means, while in work. I think of the many cases of skills that are available but being wasted: you could have somebody that is skilled at their job, knowledgeable from companies investing millions in training them to peak performance, but they're suddenly stricken. A scientist is suddenly paralysed from the waist down in a motorway crash, so do you lose the ten million pounds worth of revenue they bring in or do you make some adjustments to the working practices to keep that knowledge base?

When he was the big boxing title holder, Mike Tyson did an interview after losing a fight he was expected to win. He was asked what happened to his fight plan. He said he didn't have one. He said everyone has a plan until you get a KO punch in the face, then the plan goes out the window. And people that are lucky enough to have never gone through what I've gone through can spout their opinions because they've never been on the receiving end. When it goes wrong, it can be catastrophic. Disability is so frightening that I think people don't have the ability to think that this could happen to them at any point. But nobody's safe from this. I don't want to be a doomsayer but stepping out the front door is not the first of the day's hazards. You've got through quite a few before the working day begins.

What hampers sorting the world for the disabled is that the people legislating or governing that territory do not have that life experience, are not disabled themselves, are sitting at a desk saying we should have an elevator for this building or that office. What about someone who's got a fear of an elevator accident? There's not enough lateral thinking, it's too straightforward.

We have a Minister for Women and Equalities (Bridget Phillipson in 2025) and if that role was given to a man there'd be absolute uproar. But we've not had one disabled person as Minister for the Disabled. Which to me is strange given our sensitive environment, the world where everything must be cosmetically acceptable, where you must have the correct pronouns. Take me for instance, I'm a verbal how-do-you-do challenge.

I'm a bilateral double amputee, so I've got a physical disability. I've got one eye, so I've got a sensory impairment. I'm deaf in one ear, another sensory impairment, and I've got a mental health condition. If you look at race – black, white, Asian, mixed race – or sexual orientation – gay, straight, bi, trans, whatever it may be – you can pigeonhole it. You can't do that with disability, because I fit in eight different pigeonholes. Employers see it as too big a problem, but it isn't, it's because they are fearful of engaging with disabled people.

When I'm consulting, I tell employers all they have to offer is support to allow a successful disabled candidate in a job to make the most of the opportunity, to do the job to the fullness of their physical and mental abilities. There is a real fear in business – they don't want lawsuits – about using the wrong terms, saying the wrong thing, and being misunderstood: That's where training and intelligence come in, paying attention and doing something about it. And not being an arse – either as an employer or as a disabled person.

Talking of arses, the Department of Work and Pensions once sent me a form in regard to my disability: they wanted to know how long I could stand and how many steps I could take.

I had somebody come up to me at a conference and ask: how do I address you regarding your disability? I was astonished. Was I Danny the amputee, and over there was that Derek the deaf man and Linda the blind lady?

I said: 'I'm Dan. That's it. That's all you need. Job done.'

People must label things to make themselves feel comfortable, and it goes from the sublime to the ridiculous, where you can't challenge it. I've got no issue with anybody that wants to identify whichever way they want. That's fine. No problem with that whatsoever. I have an issue when you're telling me that I must believe what you're telling me.

I don't care what anybody wants to be, if it makes them happy, crack on and do it. But don't try to enforce that on me legally.

I like Frankie Boyle. I think he's funny but he's not everybody's cup of tea. That's fair enough but if somebody goes to a Frankie Boyle gig, and halfway through screams, 'Oh my God, I've got leprosy because Frankie Boyle offended me!'

That's absurd. If it's not a racial or homophobic slur, nothing happened, what one person finds funny somebody might find offensive. That's life. Democracy is all about everybody hearing their views. Yes, today everybody's a critic, and too many people have got used to saying stuff without getting a punch in the mouth, only because they can say it online. Which takes it into the world of being ridiculous, where you can't have a debate and challenge somebody's opinion. I can disagree with somebody and still be really good friends with them, but I feel *Big Brother* is even trying to police polite argument.

Language is a self-inflicted problem. I will refer to myself as wheelchair-bound. Not a problem, yet all the disability charities say that I'm not wheelchair-bound. I'm a wheelchair user. I'm not a disabled person. I'm a person with disabilities. It's semantics. I would never go up to somebody else and go, 'Oh, look at that cripple.' If I want to call myself a cripple, then that's up to me.

The issue with language is subjective. Everybody will identify in a different way. If you then start trying to legislate how people do that, you take away the ability to have debates and conversations, and you create greater segregation. What angers me with all this correct terminology and the furore about it every day is that's detrimental to cohesive communities.

It takes the spotlight from what I believe are real issues: people, who through horrors or sheer bad luck, can't get jobs, who live in abject poverty, who are having their benefits taken off of them and have got no social mobility.

There are more far-reaching issues, and the ongoing cosmetic nonsense is harmful. I do take it too personally because work is massive to me, it keeps me on a level footing. Still the system shoves and jostles you, people who have not been through what you have berate you and you become miserable and despondent coping with all that shit, as well as your own shit. It's asking you to be superhuman.

Even now, there are a number of organisations that do specific disability recruitment, but they don't do it well enough because they're predominantly Government-funded, so it is bums on seats, a numbers game. They do it because of the way the contract is normally structured, if they place somebody for an interview, they get paid. If that person gets a job, they get another fee. If they stay in work for three months, they get another fee. Six months, they get another fee.

If you've got a disabled person that's desperate to work, you can send them for ten jobs that you know they're never going to get. The recruitment company makes £15,000 from that, because they get £1,500 quid per interview. It's more cost effective to send them for interviews that they're not going to get, rather than have £1,500 for the interview, a grand for the first three months and a grand for the next six months.

The more interviews, the more money, it's a ludicrous situation. And the disabled person seeking work suffers disappointment and humiliation over and over again. I've got what I believe is a solution that fixes this problem but when I try and talk to the Government about it – we've had campus meetings with Government ministers in England and in Wales – it goes nowhere. I'm desperate to meet somebody new in Government to say: stop allowing businesses to hide behind bullshit. And get them to do the job they have taken responsibility for. I don't want to be a good career move for them. Still, politicians do like to pass the buck.

In my time, Dame (honoured in 2022) Maria Miller was replaced by Esther McVey and I got on well with Esther. I think she had a real good intention for the role of Minister for Disabled People, but she was in post when the Remploy factories were being closed, and she got the rough end of a really shitty stick, which she had to grab with both hands.

Sir (knighted in 2017) Mike Penning took on the responsibility and he's a brilliant individual and was a star of an MP for Hemel Hempstead until 2024. I knew Mike previously, and he was a really good minister for disabled people, and I spoke at events, and he was supportive of what we were trying to achieve. Sod's Law of course that he was good – he moved on fast to responsibility for Policing and then Justice and the Armed Forces. I tried to remain positive, even optimistic.

Justin Tomlinson took it over and we had a really good meeting, laid out all the ideas.

He enthused: 'Yeah, that's great, brilliant, brilliant. Let's take a quick photo.'

Justin Tomlinson was a marketing man turned MP, and it figured. This was in 2015, and a document had been prepared for the Government about the accessibility of football grounds and how poor the Premier League was for that. With Justin I devised a solution, a plan to make it easier for disabled fans to see their team play, and he put me in touch with the Premier League. I explained to them my ideas for access to all their 20 grounds.

We would look at where the accessible seating was, make recommendations for refurbishments, and cover every aspect, training stewards and ticket staff, and make football more welcoming for fans with difficulties. I also mapped out an online strategy about access to and into the grounds, buying tickets and even the view from your seat. With everything involved I set the price at £10,000 for each ground, a total of £200,000 for the Premier League. I sent them my proposals, organised by the Government, and still waiting for their reply.

I've met with so many UK Government ministers and

Welsh Government ministers who say: 'We will get you to do this, we will get you to do that.'

When it comes to it, nothing comes to fruition. It's all photo ops and platitudes.

Disability employment statistics haven't seen much of an increase: 0.9 % in the ten years from 2014.

What's happened is they've spent so much money on fouled things it's almost like they've gilt edged a turd. It's always about rebranding things that are soiled, giving the mess a nice new name and a snazzy new badge, but it's still the same fucking turd. And it won't flush.

Chapter Fifteen

BEDSIDE BUSINESS

'Strange, isn't it? Each man's life touches so many other lives.
When he isn't around he leaves an awful hole, doesn't he?'
– CLARENCE, IT'S A WONDERFUL LIFE, 1946

IT OFTEN FEELS LIKE tilting at windmills but each day there are small victories which crazily enough often build from setbacks. With the economic mess in 2018, accessibility took a back seat and much of my work dried up.

I was lucky to sign on with the Leonard Cheshire Disability company which has helped the disabled for more than seven decades. My job was a community-based project to support people finding a place in society, to get out of the house and do new things – find a meaning to the day. It involved developing a new online system and I got heavily into it and it was looking good.

Then Covid arrived and the pandemic instantly showed the *them and us* between the able-bodied and the disabled. I was furloughed and if my brain's not active, it goes to some really dark places, so I kept my focus watching the news, terrifying as it was seeing the Covid death toll rising, and the 'Do Not Resuscitate' notices issued to the disabled if they were taken into intensive care. I followed stories about children doing Zoom classes, but I knew that wouldn't help the neurodiverse who need personal support and were not going to interact and learn a lot via Zoom.

Unlike Mike Tyson, I had a plan. The biggest impact on the disabled community coming out of Covid was going to be education, but also employment, because Covid meant the first people out of work were the disabled staff. 7/7 changed my life forever, but just because you're disabled, it doesn't mean you can't do things. The perception of disability is the biggest stumbling block yet my inspiration and goals– and those of millions of others – are no different to anyone else's.

Within business the general attitude is 'let's not give ourselves any problems'.

There is a disability bias, maybe unconscious bias, for employers are looking for somebody that conforms to their model, that looks like them, sounds like them, behaves like them, because that's going to be the fit for the business. If somebody like me wheels into a room, generally they've got fuck all chance. They look at me and they don't see anything but a wheelchair. They don't see more than 20 years' experience. I've got multiple awards and recognition, but they just think: 'Oh, wheelchair problem.' The irony is that often they retain me as a consultant. I'm good enough to be a consultant, but I'm not good enough to work for them directly. It baffles me.

Before the pandemic, I approached a nationwide organisation about getting disabled people into their business by working from home. I was told it was not practical as it was essential employees were in the central call centre. Covid and the pandemic arrived, and staff were working from home; they, magically, found a way to make it work. I sensed an opportunity, for clearly the business carried on that way without problems. Yet, with the pandemic over, the shutters went up: no, you need to be in the office. Conformity bias once again.

Nobody, I felt, was tackling the real issue of how we apply for work and the information we need. With Gem's agreement – it was costing us money – I did an online university human resources management diploma course as part of creating a company to provide programmes for employers and work candidates. It was built on information, on transparency – a support passport to employment. A method to take away possible aggravation so the employer gets the talent they want without any hidden burden, for we are the advocate for the employee to make sure the right support is always in place. Both sides win and can focus on the job. That's the concept and we had it up and running successfully, happily complementing my efforts for all issues relating to disability and physical access working with retailers and hotels to make their buildings more accessible.

My work now includes legislation training around the Equality Act 2010, disability hate crime training, as well as helping ex-military people back into employment. We want to try to re-educate people that disability isn't something to be terrified of or brushed under the carpet. It's there and is not going away, like my PTSD and that of all the other sufferers who are fighting or hiding it.

There's still a huge stigma around mental health. Which is stupid, for that health crisis grows by the day. Watch the news. Random attacks. Families wiped out. Dads killing their children. And family embarrassment stops people seeking help?

How are you? It's one of the most disingenuous questions people ask and I very quickly realised it was loaded. When I was at that crisis point when I didn't want to be here anymore, people got default answers: 'Yeah, I'm good', 'Everything's fine.' Inside you are working out the quickest way to kill yourself. The truthful reply is: 'I've not slept for four days, I feel like shit, and I'm trying to work out how many pills and how much whisky it's going to take to kill me. But how's your day going?' They would be like: 'Oh, fuck me, that's a bit rich, and never talk to you again.'

People want the easy answer, they want you to say you're fine because when you do kill yourself, they can reveal: 'He said he was fine, how was I to know?' It makes people feel better, keeps the conscience clear.

I used to get sick and tired of playing that word game. How could I be fine after what I'd gone through? How would anybody be fine? Yet the assumption is, oh, you're physically healed up, so everything must be okay. No, I'm as broken as you can get. It's this strange social inability to deal with something different.

Every time I meet someone new, I see that singular reaction of alarm, curiosity and discomfort. That's explained as being because of my abnormal circumstances. I have a real issue with that, because I've not met one normal person in all my years. The way I am physically, the way that I live my life is my normal. My dad's normal is completely different. There isn't a normal. There is just us, and we are who we are, and we live the lives we live. To say: 'Well, you don't fit in with normal society, you must show me normal society.' People get fixated on normalcy and when you don't fit into that category, they don't know what to do or how to act.

Put mental health into the equation, and people freak out because there remains such a huge stigma about it. *Oh my god, I can't be around Dan because I might catch depression.* It doesn't work like that. It comes back to a lack of education and how incidents are reported and broadcast. They can lecture how-to-be-woke in schools but not how to cope if your mother dies when you're four years old, or things that might be helpful in terms of growing up.

It's a tough old world for everyone and ever so tricky if you step off the pavement. Imagine trying to deal with all of that on your own as many struggle to do, not only the disabled but people whose life comes up and mugs them on their head. In the 21st Century in the UK all the safety nets are gone, the social services and the hospitals dedicated to such needs. The mental health services in the UK are, and this is absurd, quite mad. If I fell out of my wheelchair and broke my arm, I wouldn't say: 'I'll wait till I break everything else and then I'll go to hospital.'

With mental health we wait until people are at crisis point before there's an intervention. And by that point, for some, it's too late, they will have committed suicide. We don't have preventive medicine as it were, but a system which acts at crisis point and that's much more expensive than intervening early, providing support and helping somebody learn a way to manage their mental illness. We wait and we wait, and we wait until people are slicing their arms or trying to kill themselves or trying to kill somebody else. There is a systematic failing of mental health provision across the country. The children that were injured in the Manchester bomb attack waited 18 months before they were assessed for CAMHS, the child adolescent mental health service.

These kids lived through a terrorist bomb attack and were put on a waiting list for help. I was a grown man, and it fucked me up. God knows what it does to a child. There should be an emergency and mental health service that kicks in when we have mass atrocities; instead, we expect people to clog their way through.

With PTSD, you only ever hear of it when somebody kills themselves with trauma, because of complex mental health issues like paranoid schizophrenia. Which is what

Valdo Calocane was suffering from when he killed three people and wounded three more in Nottingham in June 2023. He was sentenced in 2024 to be kept 'indefinitely' in a high security hospital. The victims' families were distraught by that sentence, his family equally upset that the medical establishment had allowed him to wander the streets without help despite repeated interventions.

It is an ongoing mess of a situation and, of course, reported in screaming headlines like fire engines roaring down the high street alerting people of incoming dangers. It's always the frightening situations that get attention. People don't talk about the paranoid schizophrenic who's got it under control with medication and support and works nine to five and has a family. And I understand that – news is a commercial commodity – but it creates a bogeyman that fucking terrifies people. It makes it even more difficult to have conversations around mental illness, because most people think that if you have PTSD, you are taking loads of drugs, drinking loads and/or are massively violent and aggressive. I don't do any of that, that's not in my nature, so I don't fit into society's viewpoint of what PTSD is.

The way that we portray mental illness is the Bogeyman, like Jason Voorhees of *Friday the 13th* and Michael Myers in the *Halloween* films. It's designed, like the movies, to terrify society – don't engage with such a person, they're mad. I'm not mad. I've got a mental illness brought on through trauma. It's not something that I've chosen. It's what's happened to me and doesn't make me a bad or horrible person and getting this over is important. The overriding reason for doing this book is because mental illness in the UK is so badly misunderstood. Mental health services are so damagingly under-resourced and underfunded, and people are suffering and losing their lives daily because of mental illness and mental health issues and stress and depression and so much more. There's a duty to shine a light on and show success stories where somebody has got the support and found the ability to manage their mental health even in their darkest days. That's when people need hope.

Recently, when I got to the point where I'm saying, 'I don't know if I can fucking do this anymore', I had repeated my hope mantra that tomorrow will be better, and if tomorrow's not better then the next day, the next week, the next month, because eventually, law of averages, I've got to have a good day. It's about clinging on to the good days to ride through the bad to get to the next good day. I'll tell you again and again – for it works – that Gem and I work on a ratio that if we have more good days of laughing than we do bad days of crying, we're winning. I will always reach a point sometimes where life is worse than death. And that's a scary place to be, yes, those life-worse-than-death moments. They're always in me but I've got the wherewithal to drag myself through it without Khan finally achieving victory.

The fucker came close – not that he'd ever know it – one Monday morning in 2022. I was ready for work with video calls booked in for the afternoon but around 10.30am I got this horrible taste in my mouth, like rotten eggs. I'd never sweated so much in my life; it was dripping off my fingers. I thought I'd picked up some sort of bug. But it wasn't knocking me out so I finished my calls.

I felt really, really shit and dozed off on the sofa. When I woke up, I knew I was going to be sick. I couldn't get to the bathroom, so I flew into the kitchen, grabbed a bowl, and I vomited, and it was jet black. I'd been drinking a lot of Pepsi Max lime flavour to try and kill that horrible taste in my mouth and I thought I'd thrown up the Pepsi. I had an early night, and I woke up about 2.50am needing to go to the toilet. I was drenched in sweat, the bed was soaking wet, my wheelchair was soaking wet. I transferred onto my toilet, and everything started to go. I called for Gem and as she came into the bathroom my eyes rolled back into my head, and I slumped. She grabbed me, but I'm sodden wet and she struggled to settle me before calling an ambulance.

I came round and again, threw up a load of blood, collapsed again, and when I came round the next time I was surrounded by paramedics, and I had a defibrillator on my chest. My blood pressure was way low, so there was a strong chance I was going to go into cardiac arrest, and they rushed me into hospital. My blood count had gone from 150, which is the normal level, to about 75. I'd lost about ten pints of blood. I had a camera go down, a camera go up, and the docs couldn't find anything. I was in hospital for a week. They discharged me. I was at home for a week, and I collapsed again and was rushed back in. I was in for a month, and I suffered two massive internal bleeds, something burst inside. I finally found out it was because of a change of medication – one of the side effects of the anti-depressant I'd been on for two years is it can cause internal gastro-intestinal bleeding and with me it sure did. In a big way.

It fucking upended me for it stirred up all my PTSD: I was back in hospital. I nearly died, and all from what Khan did to me, and with the nurses and hospital beds it was a rerun of what had been. I had cannulas in both arms for the blood transfusions, but the hospital left them left in too long and I was infected and my arms ballooned, I'd bulged up like Arnold Schwarzenegger. And I couldn't use them. Gem had to feed me in hospital. She'd had to wheel me to the toilet, help me on the toilet, clean me, get me back on my bed, and then feed me like I was a baby. I was desperate to keep the business going so she was dialling phone numbers for me and putting me on speaker and sending the follow-up emails.

I held some meetings from the canteen when I was wired up to a drip. You learn to get around adversity. I was more disabled than when I went into the hospital, and you have to have a black sense of humour to laugh at that unearned unhappiness. But I did.

I see the world from a different place. I don't expect you to fully go along with my thinking and I'd never want you to be in the place where you might view life through my particular 20-20 vision. You will probably find the following difficult to comprehend but here it is: If somebody came to me now with a sort of *Sophie's Choice* and said, 'Dan, I'll take you back to the 6 July 2005, you will know everything that's going to happen to you in advance, and you will have a decision to get on that train or not. If you don't get on that train, you'll never meet Gem, you'll never have your life in Wales, you'll never do all the things you've done but keep plugging on with life as it is. Or you can get on the train, go through the past 20 years, the pain, the horror, and end up where you are now. What would you do?'

I've reported to you all the negatives, and they do mount up. The positives are how life is now. 7/7 gave me a lot more than it took from me, because it gave me a new appreciation of life. It gave me an opportunity to be truly happy, which I am with Gem. It gave me an opportunity to hopefully help people that are struggling with their mental health, to raise awareness around mental health, and it's given me an opportunity to build a business to support other disabled people, to hopefully not feel the way that I did when I left hospital, as if my life was over. Yes, I'd get on the train, even knowing the shit I've gone through, because I know I'm going to come through the other side of it, yes, and be where I am now.

I can smile, and it's a genuine smile. It's not a mask I have to put on. I'm genuinely happy and I never was before. I didn't know what genuine happiness was. I do now.

It's a wonderful thing.

Chapter Sixteen

BOXING CLEVER

'A champion is someone who gets up when they can't.'
– JACK DEMPSEY, WORLD CHAMPION HEAVYWEIGHT
BOXER [1919-1926], 1957

THERE'S A TREMENDOUS MOTIVATION when you have turned your life around to want to do it for others, to spread the word– but not be over-the-top evangelical. I know only too well how you have to take it easy to help people move on from a bad place. I'm lucky to have good contacts as friends and one of them runs an amateur boxing gym. We were able to begin inclusion classes to get disabled people involved in the sport and get them a bit fitter and healthier.

We created a charity called Grand Disability Boxing, and it's centred on pad and bag work, shadow boxing and learning how to throw a punch, which is tremendous exercise and builds confidence. We branched out to schools helping kids with special educational needs. Alongside boxing, and because many of them won't ever be put forward for GCSEs, I developed a training programme of employability and enterprise skills. I'm working to get this accredited so the students can leave school with a qualification in enterprise or business.

Society is great at telling those with special educational needs or who are designated neurodiverse – where the brain works differently to the 'normal' – what they can't do. I don't know what the woke word is these days, but some physically fine people have difficulty adapting to the nine to five environment, to the rules and expectations. Nobody sits them down and says: 'What do you want to do?'

It's one of the most frustrating things, because we've helped lovely people with special needs who were told work is not viable for them. One girl was doing a catering course but was told it wouldn't result in a job because of her special needs. She comes from three generations of unemployment. She told us she couldn't work because everyone told her she couldn't work! She struggled with public transport and anxiety. I found her a job working in a kitchen and doing catering and planned to get her to and from work as part of her employment.

She's been there working full-time for two years and the chef that she works under told his bosses: 'If I ever leave, I'm taking her with me. She's one of the best young chefs I've worked with.'

Of course, that's such a good example of success and, like anyone, I like to show off the victories, but not everything works out. I use the boxing analogy for it fits the upward struggle we have: if you know that every time you step into a ring you're going to get battered and knocked on the floor, you're going to hesitate before you get in the ring; but then the bell goes and there is that fire inside you that says, 'yeah, but this might be the one where I win.'

With every beating you take, it gets harder and harder to step in the ring and if you don't try, you don't get knocked out. That's not who I am, but there are moments; you'd think after 20 years the coping mechanism would get better, but there are ongoing frustrations. Dealing with Government paperwork to process any help for the people I'm trying to get into work, having to continually confirm my own status as disabled – there's no miracle worker in the Civil Service – is an ongoing grind.

Then there are the laugh-or-cry moments. One time I went to collect a new car from the mobility vehicle dealership. I went into reception, but the car was in the showroom and there were four steps down into it. The 'sales adviser' – car salesman to you and me – arrives and explains I'll have to wheel around to a car exit-entrance. I do this in the pissing rain, and they open big sliding doors and I'm inside and getting the chat about the car. I need to go to the toilet. I've got to go back outside the building, up the ramp, into the reception section, and into the toilet which wasn't a proper accessible toilet, and I got stuck. I couldn't get up or turn around to force the door open. I'm elbowing the door trying to get attention and somebody finally freed me. I then did the lot in reverse to get back to the car. Remember, this a mobility dealership.

I contacted their HQ and suggested I produce a guide for all their *mobility* dealerships on their levels of accessibility. That hit the familiar brick wall. It was a new mobility car that almost tipped me over the edge in 2022 when everything that could go wrong seemed to be doing just that.

I picked up the car, all fine as the dealership was all one level. I drove the car home but because my driveway is on an angle I couldn't get in or out of the car from my wheelchair. I had a brand-new car on my drive that I couldn't physically use. I contacted the dealership. They said it was *mid-lease* and they could not change it. I'd had the car a fucking hour and it's mid-lease. I quite vocally explained:

'It's a three-year lease. I know it's mid-lease. Mid means middle, you...'

'Sorry, there's nothing we can do about it.'

I was forced to get the door widened and the steering wheel adjusted, which helped. I must transfer into and from the car using a banana board (a curved board used by carers to move bed-bound patients) as I can't use the car any other way. That's a first for me, a backward move, a literal pain in the ass. That car drama was one little thing. But it tickles the PTSD and makes the mind agitate to such an extent I can't appraise any day until the evening.

There's always Khan niggling away. I've got pain for the rest of my life, however long that may be. I know as I get older, as my body starts to get weaker, it's going to get more difficult. It's going to put a huge amount of pressure on Gem to take care of me and help me. That's when I dwell on Khan getting away with it scot-free, as I see it. I'm serving the life sentence he should be serving. People, honest to God, don't get how difficult living this life is. What might be trivial to some people adds up to calamity for me. We lost our cats, Reggie and Trixie, one after the other, and they had been great support for me, always around, ready for mischief or a cuddle, and the rent went up 300 quid a month. At the same time, I lost a work contract, and DWP were farting around and being difficult with the Access to Work system which allows me some support. I had a real battle going with my PTSD.

Trixie died on a Friday and Gem took her off to the vet to get her ready to take to the pet crematorium on the Monday. I was alone and distraught. We are, were, a big cat family, and lost two amazing, beautiful animals that were support animals to me.

When we lost them, it had a massive impact on me. I was heartbroken. Some might not understand the lifeline the cats were for me, but their loss heightened the frantic dis-harmony having a party in my head. I'm fighting my PTSD, bad enough when Reggie went but then we lost Trixie, and I sat in the kitchen thinking: *I knew life was going to be hard, I'm not an idiot, but this is cruel. This isn't hard. This is cruel, and I can't do it anymore.*

I laid all my medication out on the sideboard, and I was going to kill myself: two boxes of this, two boxes of that, and I was in that mindset of mixing it all up. Enough to kill me.

Fuck it. I'm done.

Yet, from somewhere sanity interrupted and I thought: *I cannot leave, I cannot do it. There is something still worth living for, and it's the life I've got with Gem.*

But for that moment in time, I couldn't see any way of making this stop other than killing myself. Each stumbling block or irritation was a minor bump in any day, but by bewildering arithmetic added up to really test my limits. Again, I reached a point where life was worse than death, and that's a horrible thing to say, and I truly believe the only reason

I'm still here now, even today, the only thing that keeps me going is Gem. If something happened to her, if she's not in my life, then I'm not having a life. I won't stick around. I wouldn't choose to do this life. I don't believe in miracles or spiritual happenings, but Gem and I met by accident, by that Facebook mix-up, and what are the chances? If we hadn't met, I'd have topped myself. No two ways about it. I know I wasn't very good at it. Again, what are the chances? Do we believe in miracles? Oh, bollocks, you have to think something's happening somewhere. Gem certainly is my guardian angel.

In 2024 I received a call out of the blue which made me realise there are others.

It was a guy called Steve, and he wanted me to do some talks around resilience and overcoming trauma for a company called Six Mental Health Solutions [SIX MHS]. We chitchatted and he said that SIX MHS was Tony Adams' company – six was Tony's Arsenal shirt number. Mr Arsenal? *The* Tony Adams, a statue outside the Emirates Stadium in north London? An England captain with 66 caps? Hundreds of appearances as centre-half and captain of Arsenal?

'Absolutely, that's him,' Steve said.

That was a full-blown fanboy moment for me. I agreed before I could agree.

We arranged an initial meeting over the Teams internet system and I dialled in for the first call about 15 minutes before the start to allow the technicians to check sound levels. I'm talking to a lady producer when suddenly Tony Adams pops up on the call. I was full fanboy, chatting about North Bank Bridge and the Armoury, and we got on well.

Twenty minutes after the session my phone pinged, and Tony had sent me a text with his contact details and got a dialogue going. Next, we're invited to Sunday lunch at his lovely house in the Cotswolds and we spent the day with him and his missus, his kids and his sister-in-law – he's such a nice, down-to-earth bloke. Afterwards, I didn't really think anything of it other than him having us to his home. It was nice of him and his wife, Poppy, and we kept in touch.

Tony founded the charitable Sporting Chance Clinic in 2000, following his personal struggles with drink and drugs, offering a range of help and treatments for sportspeople with addictions. The clinic is modelled on the Crossroads Centre rehabilitation facility founded by the rock star Eric Clapton. It's supported by an eclectic bunch of names, from Sir Elton John to Dame Kelly Holmes.

It was during Covid that Tony created Six Mental Health Solutions, which does what it says on the tin – provides mental health and addiction services to employees across a range of partnered businesses. SIX MHS today has partnerships with a string of organisations, all aimed at helping people who, for whatever reason, like me, find it hard to get through any day of the week. We were back and forth with messages, and he asked me if I fancied doing some consultancy work, and that's how it started. I went from that to running my own education department and it's grown into almost a full-time role alongside my own business.

It was a lovely upswing given the onslaught of knockbacks. It proved that even if I'm living on a cliff edge I can contribute to society and help others. Which, of course, helps stop me dropping off the cliff. SIX MHS is a very can-do outfit, all about getting on with it, finding solutions not presenting obstacles, the no-can-do attitude I've battled for two decades. Tony Adams has the personal experience and is hands-on. He confronted his problems, dealt with them, and at the same time saw there was a huge number of sportspeople with gambling, drug and alcohol addictions.

Sporting Chance acts as an in-house rehabilitation clinic and sits as a separate entity to SIX MHS. We have teams

of registered mental health nurses, therapists and coun-
sellors nationwide that people are signposted to. We've
got an addiction recovery programme, and I lead on the
education. My job is to provide training, educational
information and practical solutions around and dealing
with mental health, especially with people who have been
traumatised in some horrendous accident or some such
incident. It can happen with shock, with bereavement,
anything can shake up someone's mental health. I saw it
and experienced it during Covid, and many have still not
recovered.

I'm not employed by SIX MHS, I'm a subcontractor. I
build and deliver training and awareness campaigns SIX
feels like home for me. I do educational talks such as one
on World Suicide Prevention Day. Some of the companies
we work with have had staff so stressed out at work they're
at risk or have killed themselves. I do talks all around
the UK and introductions for mental health nurses and
doctors who offer professional medical advice. My end of
it is encouragement by example – not being put off by the
old bollocks of people and 'experts' telling you what you
can and cannot do. I've landed enough times on my arse to
understand you yourself must learn your limitations.

Everything that you know as normal, as natural, whatever
that might be, that's gone. And you have to rebuild from
ground zero. Even, as crass as it sounds, learning to get on
and off the toilet. Learning to get in and out of a car, in and
out of a shower. You go back to being a toddler, having to

learn to do all these things again. And again. Society doesn't understand that it doesn't understand what those barriers are, what those difficulties are. And for me, with the PTSD as well, with it being an alien concept to me, I didn't know how to handle it. I didn't know what these intrusive thoughts were and how I could control them. I very quickly learned that I could. I'm a very proud man, and asking for help isn't something that comes naturally to me. I saw it as a sense of weakness – that Khan won because I personally can't control my life. There are some things in life that we cannot manage on our own, we need help to get through it and there's no shame in that. When I did eventually ask for help, that's when my life started to change.

I realised very quickly that for disabled people and those who have any kind of health condition, it's not a capability issue. We don't lack the capability to do things, what we lack is the opportunity to show what we can do because of the myths and misconceptions around disability. I'm always trying to buck the trend so I looked at ways I can use my voice to try to make life better for others who've survived similar perils. Abandon the massive negative, it's so easy to get consumed in the horrors of what I saw and the physicality of what I lost. I can never get it back. My legs are gone. I'll never walk again, never climb a flight of stairs, but it's about looking at the things that I can do. And using my PTSD as a sign of strength by showing people it can be controlled. That is a huge driving force for me using my life promoting disability.

It's tough at times, it can feel like a day's work getting ready to go to work. I go out, I put a shift in, I do my job, I come home, and I do it all again tomorrow. With my PTSD, I have flashbacks, I have my terrors. Sometimes I don't sleep for long spells, but I still do what I've got to do because I'm not going to let the circumstances of what happened to me dictate how my life is. I will push against every barrier that I face.

I want to encourage people to know, whatever their trauma is, the only way out is to go through it and come out the other side. To me, the turning of trauma into triumph comes from that point onward. The moment I reached out and with Gem's encouragement asked for help, that's when I started to take control.

What Gem and I have is quite unique and quite special. We're never apart. We work together, we live together, we're together all the time and she's the better part of me. If anything ever happened to her, there would be no point in me continuing because I wouldn't want to do it without her.

Truly, I couldn't do it without her.

I firmly believe that you get one soulmate in life, and I found mine. Which has its own cruelty. When I'm in a bad place, or I'm really unwell, and I see the toll it takes on Gem, it's heartbreaking for me. The horror and the aftermath of 7/7 is my burden, and I've put that on somebody else. She loves me enough to take that and share that burden with me, but the guilt I feel is fucking immense.

Every single day I think of the ways that if I wasn't in this situation, if I was able-bodied, our life would be so much different. We'd still have the same stresses and strains as everybody else, but not magnified one million percent. When I said I'd go through it again to have Gem in my life, I would, but I don't want anyone to ever think that my heart doesn't break every single day of the week for what it does to her.

She tells me it's okay, and I know she doesn't have an issue with it, but when you love somebody as much as I love her, and I see the impact of Khan's actions on our lives it gives me pause. It's like a relay race and I'm passing her a shitty baton: the stress and upset and trauma to her when I collapsed at home and, even now, she struggles to go into our bathroom downstairs because she walked in and thought I was dead.

She thought she'd watched me die in front of her. The trauma of that, of seeing me unconscious on our bed with a defibrillator on me and paramedics doing their best and rabbiting on about cardiac arrest. It doesn't leave, and that's because of what Khan did to me. I've put that on her, and that's not fair, but again in any relationship there can be extremes of unfairness.

We all rely on other people. And are lucky if allowed to and able to. It's exacerbated for me because I've got survivor's guilt, constantly feeling unworthy of the opportunity. I would go through it all again. I really would. Overseeing construction projects, going to football training, to boxing classes, and down the pub; that was my life. That was the life of an average 20-something man. Was I going to change the world doing that? No. Do I have a slight inkling of making the world a little bit better by doing what I do now? Yes. That's what gets me out of bed every day. I wake up every morning and it's a mission.

The way that I sleep, because of the uninvited reorganising of my body, at one angle, the first thing I see when I open my eyes is my wheelchair.

Some mornings, honest to God, I don't think I can do it again, survive another day of being stuck in that fucking contraption for 19 hours, being in pain for what? But then I look the other way, and she's there, and I look at Gem and realise I can take on the world, as long as I've got her.

That's what gets me going, and I'm out of bed, and ready to go and, vitally, glad to be alive. I don't think I'm inspirational, or any of the things that people say about me; that makes me uncomfortable. The inspirational person is Adrian Heili. He risked his life to save a stranger when there was so much fear in that tunnel hanging in the air like cobwebs.

I'm alive because of the NHS. I'm alive because of Adrian. I'm alive because of Gem. I've had times in the past 20 years where I've tried to kill myself, where I've wanted to kill myself, where I've wanted to give up entirely. I don't think I'm an inspiration. I think I'm trying to make the best I can of a really shit situation. I get really frustrated when people look at disabled people who climb mountains and do parachute jumps and all the rest of it and think that's what disability is. I wouldn't jump out of a plane with legs. I'll be fucked if I'm doing it without them.

AFTERWORD

BY GEM BIDDLE

AS DAN'S WIFE, IT'S FAIR TO SAY I'VE BEEN ON ONE HELL OF A JOURney. I've seen the frustration, fear, hurt, pain, panic and sheer torment but I've also seen the smiles, the laughing and most importantly love and compassion.

You probably think I'm biased as he's my husband, but I've never met anyone in my life that has such determination to make a difference for other people through his own trauma, to constantly work through his pain and never give up, even when there are times he feels it's all too much.

I hope more than anything myself that this book will bring 7/7 back to the forefront as for too long it's been swept under the carpet, unacknowledged for whatever agenda that suits and that doesn't sit right with me. Survivors and the victims deserve to be remembered, not forgotten.

I've seen countless times how Dan touches the lives of others, people taking hope and positivity from his story, people reaching out and asking for help and it's such a powerful thing to be a part of.

I'd love to see Dan recognised for the work that he does, and I want this book to touch so many people as they go on his journey, to see that trauma can massively impact a person but that doesn't mean it has to be the end.

I'm incredibly proud to be Dan's wife and as upsetting and tough as it can be at times, I'd do it over and over again in a heartbeat. He truly is my hero!

ACKNOWLEDGEMENTS

WHERE TO START, THIS journey of writing this book would not have been possible without the passion and dedication of Douglas, Rich and Amanda, from the bottom of my heart I can't thank you enough. Not only have we written this book we have become friends who I value dearly.

To the publisher thank you for believing in this journey and believing in the need for it to be told.

To my family, 20 years since that hellish day and I know it's always there in your minds, your love and support during these 20 years has been unwavering and even in the worst times I know you were always there, although thousands of miles separate us, I love you all dearly, thank you for never giving up on me.

To Adrian and Lee, wow what can I say, firstly Lee your bravery that day defies anything I could ever compare it too, thank you my friend you are a true hero.

Adrian, I cannot begin to put into words the debt of gratitude I owe you, I literally owe you my life, in the moments after the blast I faced the worst of humanity in the bomber and the very best in you, the bravery and determination in you that day to save me and helps others lets me know these bastards will never win as long as we have people like you. The world is a better place with you in it my friend.

To the medical teams and our wonderful NHS who faced with unspeakable horrors never once gave up and fought tirelessly to keep me alive Graham the paramedic, MR Duncan Black and everyone you are heroes each and every one of you, thank you does not do justice to what you did for me, and everyone caught up in the horrors of 7/7.

And now my amazing beautiful wife Gem, for without her none of this would be possible, you my darling found a broken and damaged man, who didn't want to live anymore, you showed me kindness and love the which I believed I did not deserve, you became the light in my dark world and most of all your love gave me a reason to live, I love you more than you could ever know, and everything I am today is down to you and determination to show me there can still be joy and love in this messed up world. Gem, no you, no heartbeat.

Finally, to the 47 innocent people who lost their lives in the other blasts and their families, I am truly sorry for your loss and pain, nothing I can say will ever ease it, but you are always in my thoughts.

To Jennifer, Laura, Michael, Jonathon, Colin and David, the six innocent victims of the Edgware Road blast, my heart breaks a thousand times a day for your families, I am

ACKNOWLEDGEMENTS

so sorry there was nothing I could do in those moments after the blast to help you, to their families I am sorry that you have had to endure 20 years of pain and injustice and I am so, so sorry for your loss.

ABOUT THE AUTHORS

DAN BIDDLE remains as gregarious as he was as a 19-stone, 6ft 4in construction site manager and semi-professional football goalkeeper. Everything else in his life changed when he got on the second carriage of a Tube train at Liverpool Street station in 2005. In the past decades, while dealing with his injuries, he has become an advocate for the disabled and a vocal campaigner giving talks and presentations to Government and local authorities about what more can be done to help the physically disadvantaged. He has appeared on television many times in this role. In 2019 he began working with the Leonard Cheshire Trust helping those with disabilities like himself to live as independently as they possibly can. He maintains he is in ongoing recovery from the trauma he suffered and believes telling his story in full for the first time, with all its personal indignities and momentary defeats, will be like a gospel for the millions, like him, for whom every day is a challenge but who want to fight on.

ABOUT THE AUTHORS

DOUGLAS THOMPSON is the *Sunday Times* bestselling author of many non-fiction books covering an eclectic mix of subjects from major Hollywood biographies to revelatory bestsellers about remarkable people and events. Four of his books are at present being developed for global television, another for film in Hollywood. His collaboration, *Devil's Coin*, was shortlisted for the Crime Writers Association (CWA) 2024 Golden Dagger for non-fiction. With Christine Keeler, he wrote her revealing memoir *The Truth At Last*. That instant bestseller was revised as *Secrets and Lies: The Trials of Christine Keeler* and the audio version recorded by actress Sophie Cookson who played Christine to critical acclaim in the successful BBC television series. His works, published in a dozen languages, include the television-based anthology *Hollywood People*, and worldwide selling biographies of Clint Eastwood, Madonna and John Travolta. He collaborated with Michael Flatley on the bestseller *Lord of the Dance*. Recent success came with *Inside Out: The Extraordinary Legacy of April Ashley* which was named a London *Daily Telegraph* 2024 Book of the Year He divides his time between a medieval Suffolk village and California, where he lived as a Fleet Street correspondent and columnist for more than 20 years.

www.dougiethompson.com.
@dougiethompson